99 BIBLE
CROSSWORD PUZZLES

© 2014 by Barbour Publishing, Inc.

Crosswords were created using licensed Crossword Weaver software (www.crosswordweaver.com).

Puzzles were prepared by Patricia Mitchell and Laura Lisle, in association with Snapdragon Group, Tulsa, Oklahoma, USA.

Print ISBN 978-1-68322-754-0

Published by Barbour Books, an imprint of Barbour Publishing, Inc., 1810 Barbour Drive, Uhrichsville, Ohio 44683, www.barbourbooks.com

Our mission is to inspire the world with the life-changing message of the Bible.

 Member of the
Evangelical Christian
Publishers Association

Printed in China.

99 BIBLE CROSSWORD PUZZLES

BARBOUR BOOKS
An Imprint of Barbour Publishing, Inc.

PARABLES OF JESUS

ACROSS

1 Turn the other one if slapped
6 "In laughter the heart may __" (Prov. 14:13 NIV)
10 Keyboard key
13 Be not just this, but 25 Down also
15 Jesus anointed blind man's eyes with this
16 Golfer's need
17 Cleopatra's love
18 "I am the __, ye are the branches" (John 15:5)
19 La Brea pits content
20 Lydia worked with them (Acts 16)
22 "__ us our debts"
24 Thought
26 Record player
28 Mined metals
29 The __ Samaritan
30 Some rest stop rooms
31 Passes at the bull
32 "Pay back what you __ me!" (Matt. 18:28 NIV)
33 "We have __ his star in the east" (Matt. 2:2)
34 Deli order
35 Tavern owner
37 Along 43 Across
41 "__ your light so shine" (Matt. 5:16)
42 Sight on 43 Across
43 __ of Galilee
44 Psychologist Sigmund
47 He builds his house on sand
48 Jesus' mom
49 Season before Easter
50 "Let these sayings __ down into your ears" (Luke 9:44)
51 Indiana city
52 How some described Jesus
54 Decorative needle case
56 Female parent (var.)
57 "This night thy __ shall be required of thee" (Luke 12:20)
59 Supple
63 Barely make it (with "out")
64 Old story
65 A man "shall __ unto his wife" (Gen. 2:24)
66 Take out (Abbr.)
67 Fencer's need
68 Sharp as a two-__ sword

DOWN

1 Repeated, a dance
2 "Even as a __ gathereth her chickens" (Matt. 23:37)
3 Do this at a feast
4 Worn
5 Safari destination
6 Hovercraft (Abbr.)
7 Dover's are white
8 Vietnamese capital
9 Ogler
10 Raiment
11 "Beware of the __ of the Pharisees" (Mark 8:15)
12 Mother __ of India
14 Bread choice
21 They will be separated from 23 Down
23 They will be separated from 21 Down
24 Hawkeye State

25 See 13 Across

27 29 Across took the wounded
man to one

29 Lump

30 "Bring forth...fruits __ for repentance" (Matt. 3:8)

31 Ado

33 What the sower sowed

34 Plague woe

36 Clumsy one

37 What thorns did to some 33
Down

38 Russian ruler

39 Ethereal

40 "Now I __ me down to sleep"

42 The Prodigal __

44 Blazed

45 Create again

46 Tooth layer

47 "Go __!"

48 They're called to the feast
(Luke 14:13)

50 Spy

51 Duplicity

53 Caribbean sight

55 Tenderness (Abbr.)

58 Downwind

60 Judas carried one (John
13:29)

61 First Lady

62 Esau's color (Gen. 25:25)

2
MIRACLES OF JESUS

ACROSS

1 Lingerie item
4 Certain grieving mother in Nain (Luke 7:12)
9 Brazilian dance
14 Umpire, for short
15 Filipino dish
16 Greek epic poem
17 Jesus restored Malchus's (Luke 22:51)
18 Open the door for (2 words)
19 "It is hard for you to kick against the __" (Acts 26:14 NIV)
20 49th state
22 "Thy will be __"
24 Salon service
25 "One __ him an hundred pence" (Matt. 18:28)
27 Location
31 Jekyll's alter ego
32 One who watched Jesus' tomb
33 Jesus died to cleanse this
34 Mites equivalent
36 Bundled hay
38 Jesus raised his daughter (Mark 5:22)
40 One of many at Lazarus's tomb
42 Locale of one miracle
43 Language of India
44 Choose
45 Make amends for sin
47 Flightless birds
51 "I will give unto thee the __ of the kingdom" (Matt. 16:19)
53 "Why did the heathen __?" (Acts 4:25)
54 See 40 Down
55 Printer needs

57 Went to the gas pump
59 One of many in Proverbs
62 Long stories
65 He brought five loaves and two fish (John 6:9)
66 "The __ of the body is the eye" (Matt. 6:22)
67 Tests
68 Expert suffix
69 Hot dog alternatives
70 Only one thanked Jesus (Luke 17:12–15)
71 There were this many of 70 Across

DOWN

1 "Ye shall know my __ of promise" (Num. 14:34)
2 KJV's verily
3 "It is I; be not __" (Matt. 14:27)
4 What Jesus does on 42 Across
5 Brainstorm result
6 URL feature
7 Kimono sash
8 Doing 42 Across was one
9 Healing 70 Across was one
10 Lotion ingredients
11 "Mama __!"
12 They "cast the __ away" (Matt. 13:48)
13 TV spots
21 Denarii, for example
23 Not even
25 Exits
26 "Is, __, and always will be"
28 Aegean Sea feature
29 Level
30 "World without __"

32 African antelope
35 Sin
36 "Take up thy __, and walk" (John 5:8)
37 Each one (2 words)
38 Jest
39 Courtroom figure (Abbr.)
40 Jesus changed water into this at 54 Across
41 Opposite of WSW
42 Stir fry cooker
43 Sow's mate
45 Noah's vessel
46 Mortarboard feature
48 Gavel
49 Anxiety
50 Make sorrowful
52 Jesus restored this for many

56 "Let down your __ for a draught" (Luke 5:4)
57 Jesus' miracles brought Him a lot of this
58 Old federation
59 Priest's vestment
60 Manager (Abbr.)
61 Turkish title
63 "The __ is laid unto the root of the trees" (Luke 3:9)
64 "I had rebuilt the wall and not a __ was left in it" (Neh. 6:1 NIV)

3
FIRST CHRISTIANS

ACROSS

1 Hair locale
6 Volcano spew
10 Data storage devices
13 Made neater
15 Car rental agency
16 Sower's need
17 One devil possessed, biblically
18 Scam
19 Take flight
20 Do not do this concerning good works
22 24 Across's mentor
24 Former persecutor of Christians
26 Dr. Zhivago's love
28 Norwegian capital
29 Prays
30 Bethany follower of Jesus
31 Church table
32 Miner's find
33 Place for hats, maybe
34 Sports ministry org. (Abbr.)
35 Wind-powered apparatus
37 "Thou shalt be his __ unto all men" (Acts 22:15)
41 Long, long time
42 Trespasses
43 __ Grande
44 Emission
47 Turfs
48 Eutychus's seat (Acts 20:9)
49 You can whistle a happy one
50 Late-night host Jay
51 "My people are __ to backsliding from me" (Hos. 11:7)
52 Aaron's son

54 "Faith cometh by hearing, and hearing by the __ of God" (Rom. 10:17)
56 Watchdog agency
57 Humorist Bombeck
59 Do not let your faith do this
63 Insult, slangily
64 Good fight of faith, for example
65 In Jerusalem were "devout men, out of every __ under heaven" (Acts 2:5)
66 Hog's home
67 "I have neither __ on usury" (Jer. 15:10)
68 Compact

DOWN

1 Bible scholar's degree, maybe (Abbr.)
2 Spy org. (Abbr.)
3 Sum up
4 Edge in science
5 Do not cast one before swine
6 Ten Commandments, for example
7 Bird sanctuary
8 Lithuanian capital
9 24 Across often went there
10 __ died for us
11 Cameroon seaport
12 Detector
14 Genetic code
21 Frozen dessert
23 "Ryan Express" baseballer
24 South American nation
25 Teen suffix
27 Noah's float

29 Automated tasker, for short
30 German novelist Thomas
31 Bible book written by Luke
33 Response to 24 Across' preaching, often
34 Fish features
36 City of studious Christians (Acts 17:10–11)
37 Often neglected woman in Acts 6:1
38 Ireland
39 Nile Delta element
40 Sun (Lat.)
42 "He...spared not his own __" (Rom. 8:32)
44 "Harness the horses, mount the __!" (Jer. 46:4 NIV)
45 Pastor's place

46 Fearful
47 Sunday morning oration
48 Stately
50 24 Across audience size, often
51 Communion element
53 Missionary need
55 "Considerest not the beam that is in thine __ eye?" (Matt. 7:3)
58 "Go to the __, thou sluggard" (Prov. 6:6)
60 Relation
61 VW model
62 SSW opposite

4

NEW TESTAMENT WOMEN

ACROSS

1 Queen of __, Solomon's visitor
6 Diminishes
10 Traffic snarl
13 Lava product
15 Train station (Fr.)
16 They did this at the Last Supper
17 Broker's account, maybe
18 Elation
19 "If the salt loses __ saltiness" (Matt. 5:13 NIV)
20 Bible pronoun
22 Martha's brother
24 What a woman brought to a judge in Luke 18:3 NIV
26 Hurried
28 Sinai sight
29 Many 50 Downs in Jesus' time
30 What Mary wiped with her hair
31 Smelled
32 __ Baba
33 Joppa, for one
34 Scratch
35 Limits
37 Jezebel "__ her face" (2 Kings 9:30)
41 Little bit
42 Swiss canton capital
43 Early Christianity, with "the"
44 Engine
47 Bethany, for one
48 50 down's offering
49 How the women found Jesus' tomb
50 Decrease
51 "The __ eat of the crumbs" (Matt. 15:27)
52 Satan to Jesus, for example

54 Baseball's Nolan
56 Economic measure (Abbr.)
57 Eve's hubby
59 "Evil...the sort of error that __ from a ruler" (Eccl. 10:5 NIV)
63 Wing
64 Lots
65 Links together
66 Deli choice
67 Lush valley in Pakistan
68 Fuse ores

DOWN

1 Caesarea to Bethany (dir.)
2 "The kingdom of heaven __ come near" (Matt. 10:7 NIV)
3 Keyboard key
4 Trade
5 Island greeting
6 "Ask an __, will he offer him a scorpion?" (Luke 11:12)
7 Dance
8 Martha's kitchen creation
9 Online adieu
10 Jesus raised his daughter
11 Adjust
12 Dirties, with "up"
14 Double
21 Manual readers
23 "Women __ themselves in modest apparel" (1 Tim. 2:9)
24 Fiery serpent's holder
25 Timothy's grandma
27 Fluffy or Fido
29 Buddy
30 Affectionate
31 Jesus raised widow's son from the dead here

33 Partridge's tree, in song
34 Martha's sister
36 "He that is without sin...first cast a __ at her" (John 8:7)
37 Jesus healed his mother-in-law
38 Branch
39 "Whoever __ this bread will live forever" (John 6:51 NIV)
40 Lydia's business need
42 Container
44 Peddler
45 Jesus taught this way
46 Jerusalem center of worship
47 Yellow melon
48 Philosophical belief opposite of Pluralism
50 See 48 Across
51 Challenges
53 Droops

55 Thanksgiving vegetable
58 Colorado winter hour
60 "__ shall bring forth a son" (Matt. 1:21)
61 Conger
62 Former JFK lander (Abbr.)

NEW TESTAMENT MEN

ACROSS

1 "__, our eye hath seen it" (Ps. 35:21)
4 Governing group
9 "We spend our years as __ that is told" (Ps. 90:9) (2 words)
14 9 Down daily task
15 "Not __ your liberty for a cloke of maliciousness" (1 Peter 2:16)
16 One returned to thank Jesus
17 Anger
18 The Nile has one
19 Unite
20 Winter storm need
22 Plant fiber
24 Sicilian spewer
25 Self-satisfied
27 __ priest, 67 Across position
31 Italian duke
32 Definitely not cool
33 Flapper's accessory
34 Caleb, for one
36 Disgust
38 Place of prayer
40 Confront
42 Grasslands
43 Greek philosopher
44 "The wise took __ in their vessels" (Matt. 25:4)
45 "Seest thou a man that is __ in his words" (Prov. 29:20)
47 Dart
51 Black gem
53 "Jesus...went up __ a mountain to pray" (Luke 9:28 NIV)
54 Opera solo
55 What Caleb did in the Promised Land

57 Peter's brother
59 Car make
62 Segment
65 The New Testament is one
66 Simon of Cyrene's son
67 See 27 Across
68 __ Lanka
69 66 Across's dad bore it for Jesus
70 "My wife well stricken in __" (Luke 1:18)
71 Elephant's name

DOWN

1 Stayed with
2 David's "tomb is __ this day" (Acts 2:29 NIV) (2 words)
3 Graying
4 New Testament book writer
5 Consumer
6 Nada
7 Explosive (Abbr.)
8 Prophet in Acts 11:28
9 "He...sat for __ at the Beautiful gate" (Acts 3:10)
10 Gnashing of __
11 Easter month, sometimes (Abbr.)
12 Lower limb
13 "Sir, come down __ my child die" (John 4:49)
21 Roman ruler
23 "He is of __; ask him" (John 9:23)
25 Paul's former name
26 Arizona winter hour
28 Wading bird
29 Inflammatory disease
30 Noah's son
32 "Tell-Tale Heart" writer

35 U.S. Census data (Abbr.)
36 Fall month (Abbr.)
37 Thingamabob
38 A mite, for example
39 __ Spirit
40 Choir section
41 Sandy island (var.)
42 Cow sound
43 Oregon winter hour
45 Bunny move
46 "Don't let anyone deceive you in __" (2 Thess. 2:3 NIV) (2 words)
48 Soldiers came to __ Jesus
49 __ Nevada range
50 Pacific state
52 African ground squirrel
56 Talk back
57 Seaweed substance

58 Loch __ monster
59 Spark
60 Mutt
61 Alien's craft (Abbr.)
63 Compass point
64 Biological instructions carrier (Abbr.)

ACROSS

1 Poets
6 Long story
10 Medical group (Abbr.)
13 "I will give you thirty __ and thirty change of garments" (Judges 14:12)
15 Saudi citizen
16 "He be not __ from every one of us" (Acts 17:27)
17 Engine element
18 Food, informally
19 Weekday (Abbr.)
20 49 Across condition
22 Husband of Sapphira
24 "Jesus Christ, by __ we have now received the atonement" (Rom. 5:11)
26 "Veil of the temple was __ in twain" (Matt. 27:51)
28 Data, for short
29 64 Across greeting
30 "Witness...of what thou __ seen and heard" (Acts 22:15)
31 Luster
32 Sun's name
33 The __ Supper
34 Lyric verse
35 Erratic
37 Transport
41 Sleep stage (Abbr.)
42 Was blinded on the road
43 "Disciples were filled with __" (Acts 13:52)
44 Relieved
47 "Who hath known the __ of the Lord?" (Rom. 11:34)
48 Wind pointer

49 "He which sat for __ at the Beautiful gate" (Acts 3:10)
50 "He gave her his __, and lifted her up" (Acts 9:41)
51 Pentecost's tongues of __
52 "The __ shall come to poverty" (Prov. 23:21)
54 Agabus was one
56 "They __ him...into Damascus" (Acts 9:8)
57 Embraces
59 Nix
63 "If he shall ask an __, will he offer him a scorpion?" (Luke 11:12)
64 42 Across was often this
65 Manuscript checker
66 Golfer's accessory
67 "I would thou __ cold or hot" (Rev. 3:15)
68 Show scorn

DOWN

1 U.K. August hours
2 Expression of surprise
3 Agent, for short
4 Send abroad, maybe
5 Vapor
6 Hang down
7 Complete
8 Tense
9 Aramaic daddy
10 Elizabeth and Mary's relationship, for one
11 Pitcher
12 Where Paul and Silas were put
14 Theologian's degree (Abbr.)
21 Eliminate

23 __ habet (Lat.)
24 Horse's command
25 __ Ghost
27 NYC winter time
29 Tree
30 "He shook off the beast...and felt no __" (Acts 28:5)
31 42 Across's former name
33 Sin of 22 Across and his wife
34 "__ him, all ye people" (Rom. 15:11)
36 Grab
37 "Then laid they their __ on them" (Acts 8:17)
38 Slightly open
39 "Her masters saw...the hope of their gains was __" (Acts 16:19)
40 Eyeball
42 Fasten

44 Baby bird, maybe
45 Assert
46 Blur
47 Jesus' birth bed
48 __ Mary
50 Simon's __, where Peter saw a vision
51 Consumes food
53 Melt
55 Chemistry suffix
58 Day after 19 Across (Abbr.)
60 "I took the little book...and __ it up" (Rev. 10:10)
61 Foot digit
62 Sin

BOOK OF REVELATION

ACROSS

1 Church bell sound
5 "__ of every unclean...bird" (Rev. 18:2)
9 Location of seven churches
13 Pathway
14 Worthy is the __
15 Connect, in a way
16 "Partridge sitteth on __" (Jer. 17:11)
17 "Fire was cast __ the sea" (Rev. 8:8)
18 Navy's place (2 words)
19 "__ is he that readeth" (Rev. 1:3)
21 Nothing
23 Conger
24 Ephesus to Troas (dir.)
25 "Phantom of the Opera" author
29 Laodiceans weren't this
30 "Jesus __" (John 11:35)
32 SSW opposite
33 Tool shop element
36 Not lows
37 "__, thou knowest" (Rev. 7:14)
38 "Even to __ hairs will I carry you" (Isa. 46:4)
39 Italian city
40 Jesus' disciple, familiarly
41 Tidal movement
42 National symbols
43 34 Down tokens, perhaps
44 Time period
45 40 Across's work need
46 Point
47 Where John received his vision
49 "I make all things __" (Rev. 21:5)
50 Horse food
53 "I __ overcame" (Rev. 3:21)

55 In abundance
57 Censer's emission
60 What gold bricks in heaven do
62 Over
63 Bound
64 First garden
65 Pitch
66 Four beasts were full of them
67 See 29 Across
68 Rushed

DOWN

1 Trainee
2 One of the beasts was like this
3 Messenger to John
4 "Who am __ than the least of all saints" (Eph. 3:8)
5 Patron
6 Root beer brand (3 wds.)
7 U.K. time zone
8 Black
9 John saw a gold one
10 Mary to Martha, for short
11 Sorbet
12 Wanted poster letters (Abbr.)
15 Police academy enrollee
20 Jesus' head compared to this
22 "I am __ and Omega" (Rev. 1:8)
26 Beginning
27 "__ my heart to fear thy name" (Ps. 86:11)
28 Former name of Jerez
29 "A golden cup in __ hand full of abominations" (Rev. 17:4)
30 Angels' features
31 Many celebrities have big ones
33 God's flock
34 Indian snake

35 Moroccan capital
36 If you have ears, do this
39 "Sea of __ like unto crystal" (Rev. 4:6)
40 Revelation's bottomless __
42 Scammed
43 Plague dispenser in Revelation
46 Require
48 Orders
49 Innie or outie locale
50 "Jacob took the stone...and poured oil __ of it" (Gen. 28:18 NIV) (2 words)
51 Compensate for, as sins
52 Used a keyboard
54 Oil cartel (Abbr.)
56 Jesus does this with sinners

57 Teresa, Clare, or Anne (Abbr.)
58 Mother's Day month
59 Unlocked (poet.)
61 Hoopla

PAUL'S LETTERS

ACROSS

1 What a gossip does
5 Eye infection
9 Certain groundhog
13 "We...should walk in newness of __" (Rom. 6:4)
14 "Redeem them __ were under the law" (Gal. 4:5)
15 Where Paul left Titus
16 Leave out
17 "I had no __ in my spirit" (2 Cor. 2:13)
18 Cleanse, in a way
19 He was saved by faith
21 Rock of __
23 Digit
24 "If the whole body were an __" (1 Cor. 12:17)
25 Pauline epistle
29 Booking (Abbr.)
30 "I press on toward the __" (Phil. 3:14 NIV)
32 Opposed to gospel, in Paul's epistles
33 Strong rope fiber
36 Support
37 Even score
38 "As in __ all die" (1 Cor. 15:22)
39 Wooden box
40 Subject of 1 Corinthians 13
41 Weekday (Abbr.)
42 "Ye heard the word of __" (Eph. 1:13)
43 Paul's preaching did this to some people
44 "__ things are passed away" (2 Cor. 5:17)
45 Small particle

46 Gray sea eagle
47 Equity
49 Irritate (sl.)
50 Montana winter hour
53 "We __ should walk in newness of life" (Rom. 6:4)
55 Religious recluse
57 "Are you not __ of what the law says?" (Gal. 4:21 NIV)
60 Convex shape
62 Actor Alda
63 "Diversities of __, but the same Spirit" (1 Cor. 12:4)
64 Chicken house
65 Job's clothes, at one time
66 Inscribe
67 One of three in 1 Corinthians 13
68 "At the name of Jesus every __ should bow" (Phil. 2:10)

DOWN

1 Swell
2 State of uncertainty
3 Hell is said to be this
4 Greek letter
5 Drifts away
6 Subject matter
7 Affirmatives (sl.)
8 Gospel singer James
9 Rainbow maker
10 "As a __ gathereth her chickens" (Matt. 23:37)
11 "The world through __ wisdom did not know him" (1 Cor. 1:21 NIV)
12 Downwind
15 Some Louisianans

20 "Thou shalt bruise his __" (Gen. 3:15)
22 "The __ of our Lord Jesus Christ" (Rom. 16:20)
26 Choir section
27 Gullible
28 "We are unto God a __ savour of Christ" (2 Cor. 2:15)
29 Sacrificed instead of Isaac
30 Persona non __
31 God swore one to Abraham
33 South Pacific island nation
34 Paul condemned these
35 __ of time
36 Men's fragrance
39 Paul preached the __ of Christ
40 Medical caregiver (Abbr.)
42 "I know not to give flattering __" (Job 32:22)

43 Strongly encourage
46 Vacation destination, maybe
48 "Things above, not on things on the __" (Col. 3:2)
49 Jazz style
50 Italian city
51 Sermon site, maybe
52 Taut
54 "That hurts!"
56 Paul's once-rejected companion
57 This present __
58 Clever fellow
59 Athletic group (Abbr.)
61 Pasture sound

GOSPEL OF MATTHEW

ACROSS

1 What Jesus calmed in Matthew 8
5 Fake chocolate
10 Pay __
13 Where Paul preached in Greece, often
15 Auto make
16 __ Baba
17 "__ of me" (Matt. 11:29)
18 "I send you forth as __ in the midst of wolves" (Matt. 10:16)
19 Swine
20 They "__ him away to crucify him" (Matt. 27:31)
21 Enter at the straight __
23 "Go...and __ all nations" (Matt. 28:19)
25 One descended at Jesus' baptism
26 Fryer
28 Changeable
31 Rationalism
32 "Phantom of the __"
33 "Come unto me...and I will give you __" (Matt. 11:28)
34 Gravestone letters
37 Paul would have made one
38 What 52 Across does
40 "His __ did shine as the sun" (Matt. 17:2)
41 The __ of the world, Matthew 24 subject
42 Tropical bird
43 Strongly suggests
44 Oregon capital
45 Bogus
46 Snacks for 9 Down
49 Fool built a house on it
50 Where Mary and Joseph fled
51 Bog
52 "Ears to hear, __ him hear" (Matt. 11:15)
55 Gentleness (Abbr.)
56 Anesthetic
59 "Ye __ the violence of your hands" (Ps. 58:2)
61 Hair product
62 Recycle
63 "When Cyrenius was governor of __" (Luke 2:2)
64 "__ to Joy"
65 Jesus' tempter
66 Star position

DOWN

1 Offered to Jesus on the cross
2 "African Queen" screenwriter James
3 "Each one should carry their own __" (Gal. 6:5 NIV)
4 Fall into sin
5 Social position
6 Hurt
7 Herb Pharisees would tithe
8 Unrefined metal
9 John the __
10 Of the Vatican
11 Wonderland girl
12 Don't hide yours under a bushel
14 African nation
22 "__ Maria"
24 Tree
25 "I did cast them out as the __ in the streets" (Ps. 18:42)
26 What the sower sows
27 Judas betrayed Jesus with one
28 What's we see in our brother's eye

29 Jesus' tomb on the third day
30 Flex
31 "Being warned of God in a __"
   (Matt. 2:12)
34 Prego's competition
35 57 Down choice
36 Mexican money
38 "How long __ ye between two
   opinions?" (1 Kings 18:21)
39 "Their __ were opened"
   (Matt. 9:30)
40 Flintstone man
42 You can't serve two
43 "__ and World Report"
44 "I will come in...and will __
   with him" (Rev. 3:20)
45 Average, on the golf course
46 Free (2 words)
47 Eyed

48 Rotation
49 Signal
51 Plateau
52 Old Italian money
53 Sponsorship
54 "Where is he __ is born
   King of the Jews?"
   (Matt. 2:2)
57 Beverage
58 Hovel
60 The light of the body, in
   Matthew 6:22

GOSPEL OF MARK

ACROSS

1 What multitudes sat on in Mark 6
6 Pre-K lessons
10 Relaxation site
13 IRS cases
15 "Peace of God __ in your hearts" (Col. 3:15)
16 Shade tree
17 Ridges
18 "Learn a parable of the fig __" (Mark 13:28)
19 Music genre
20 Preach the Good __
22 What John did to Jesus
24 They "rolled a stone unto the __ of the sepulchre" (Mark 15:46)
26 Potter's oven
28 "This is my beloved Son: __ him" (Mark 9:7)
29 "First the blade, then...the full __ in the ear" (Mark 4:28)
30 Adorable
31 Trench
32 Angelus word
33 What Jesus forgave
34 Jesus "put forth __ hand" (Mark 1:41)
35 Request a favor, maybe
37 Tangled
41 Lion name
42 One might be drawn in the sand
43 Noah's craft
44 Tapestry
47 Wide road (Abbr.)
48 Former Russian ruler
49 It will not give light at End Times (Mark 13:24)

50 Game cubes
51 Rents to
52 "No man putteth new wine into old __" (Mark 2:22)
54 Paper package
56 Behind
57 "Take thine ____, eat, drink..." (Luke 12:19)
59 Attach
63 Exclamation of wonderment
64 "My beloved is like...a young __" (Songs 2:9 NIV)
65 Secret revealer
66 Gray sea eagle
67 One who accosted the traveler in Luke 10
68 Southpaw

DOWN

1 Mary or Martha (sl.)
2 Regret
3 Who "can __ one cubit unto his stature?" (Matt. 6:27)
4 Join (2 words)
5 Drive
6 KJV verb
7 Brook sound
8 "Thou canst make me __" (Mark 1:40)
9 Leak slowly
10 The World __
11 Fountain sites, often
12 Current unit
14 Opposite of NNE
21 Smelly mammal
23 "It came to pass in __ days" (Mark 1:9)
24 It descended from heaven when 22 Across took place

25 Mined metals
27 If salt "loses __ saltiness" (Mark 9:50 NIV)
29 Semi feature
30 "See ya later!"
31 Number loaves when 1 Across took place
33 Blind man does this after Jesus heals him
34 "Kingdom of God is at __" (Mark 1:15)
36 "Sow the fields, and __ vineyards" (Ps. 107:37)
37 The Jordan __
38 __ Days, subject of Mark 13
39 Time periods
40 Danish currency (Abbr.)
42 Business ending (Abbr.)
44 Winding path
45 Shingler

46 "The seed is __ under their clods" (Joel 1:17)
47 Guinea-__, West African nation
48 Where Jesus cast out moneychangers
50 "My soul is exceeding sorrowful unto __" (Mark 14:34)
51 Place for a boutonniere
53 "Take heed __ any man deceive you" (Mark 13:5)
55 John "did __ locusts and wild honey" (Mark 1:6)
58 Omelette ingredient
60 Santa's helper
61 Need for Peter and Andrew in Mark 1
62 "They passed through the Red sea as by __ land" (Heb. 11:29)

GOSPEL OF LUKE

ACROSS

1 Slightly open
5 School groups (Abbr.)
9 "Your feet __ with the preparation of the gospel" (Eph. 6:15)
13 "Though I be __ in speech" (2 Cor. 11:6)
14 The __ Supper
15 "Son of man cometh at an hour when ye __ not" (Luke 12:40)
16 Citrus drinks
17 Shaft
18 Jesus changed it into wine
19 What John came to do
21 "Blessed are ye that __ now" (Luke 6:21)
23 Former speedy transport (Abbr.)
24 Wicked
25 Ruffles
29 Sneer at
30 Tel __
32 Lion moniker
33 Goliath's foe
36 God's freely given mercy
37 The Ten Commandments, e.g.
38 Opposed to (dial.)
39 Christian symbol
40 Jesus' foster dad (Sp.)
41 Tax agency
42 Oozy substance
43 "His word was with __" (Luke 4:32)
44 "__ us now go even unto Bethlehem" (Luke 2:15)
45 Abba
46 Mother's Day month
47 Easter celebrations, e.g.
49 Jesus, __of God

50 "__ brought forth a son" (Luke 1:57)
53 Serpent sound
55 Dealt with
57 Shiny fabric
60 "What's the bright __?"
62 "Let him impart to him that hath __" (Luke 3:11)
63 Bias
64 Pinches
65 Standard
66 "Who can __ war against it?" (Rev. 13:4 NIV)
67 "Your Father, who __ what is done in secret" (Matt. 6:4 NIV)
68 Capital of Western Samoa

DOWN

1 Many in the Middle East
2 Jesus' betrayer
3 Skillful
4 "Come unto me...I will give you __" (Matt. 11:28)
5 Public squares
6 "All the world should be __" (Luke 2:1)
7 Certain communication (Abbr.)
8 What Jacob fed his famished brother
9 Form
10 "Prophesy! Who __ you?" (Luke 22:64 NIV)
11 Three Persons, __ God
12 Danish currency (Abbr.)
15 Disciple number
20 Footnote abbreviation (Lat.)
22 Long stories

26 "Ye bear witness that ye __ the deeds of your fathers" (Luke 11:48)
27 Taunt
28 Parable subject with seeds
29 Great noise
30 Pleasant smell
31 Flower holder
33 Our __ bread
34 "__ with thine adversary quickly" (Matt. 5:25)
35 Former Microsoft product
36 Certain stagehand
39 Potter's needs
40 "Good tidings of great __" (Luke 2:10)
42 Treatment for a broken bone
43 Window feature
46 Mire

48 European river
49 Cliff (arch.)
50 "Latchet of whose shoes I am not worthy to __ down and unloose" (Mark 1:7)
51 ___ Matisse, painter
52 Swelling
54 "Thy __ are forgiven thee" (Luke 5:20)
56 She saw Baby Jesus in the temple
57 Compass dir.
58 Pie __ mode (2 words)
59 Name in a photo
61 What Jesus does on Calvary

GOSPEL OF JOHN

ACROSS

1 Prayer word
5 Gulf war missile
9 Sinai landscape descriptor
13 Chocolate candy name
14 Trial situation
15 Fashion
16 Paul's missionary destination
17 Flair
18 Easter morning messenger
19 Where Jesus raised Lazarus from death
21 Community org. (Abbr.)
23 Caesarea to Jerusalem (dir.)
24 King (Lat.)
25 Caesarea has one
29 Sneer at (slang)
30 Lazarus "had __ in the grave four days" (John 11:17)
32 Climate watchdog group (Abbr.)
33 "I am the __ of life (John 6:35)
36 Paul, "the __ of sinners" (1 Tim. 1:16 NIV)
37 "I saw thee under the __ tree" (John 1:50)
38 "Behold the __ of God" (John 1:29)
39 Toss out
40 What Jesus changed water into
41 "__ to a Grecian Urn"
42 Some UK dwellers
43 Musical tones
44 Peter's trade tool
45 Slimy
46 Manna came with it
47 Wood nymphs
49 Toddler
50 See 44 Across

53 Payment option
55 Bring into bondage
57 Tempter
60 Lazarus's tomb, probably
62 Maintain
63 "He that is without sin...let him first cast a __ at her" (John 8:7)
64 Ointment brought to Jesus' tomb
65 Not women's
66 "__ of this body" (2 Peter 1:13 NIV)
67 Jesus' mom
68 "Or __ believe me for the very works' sake (John 14:11)

DOWN

1 Many Holy Land dwellers
2 Law-giver of old
3 Scribes and Pharisees in Jesus' time, e.g.
4 Old Testament ship builder
5 Easter play sections
6 Sepals of a flower
7 Red, white, and blue nation (Abbr.)
8 What Peter did three times
9 Measuring instrument
10 "If he...ask an __, will he offer him a scorpion?" (Luke 11:12)
11 What Peter would do after 8 Down
12 Conger
15 Empty
20 Sinai descriptor
22 Carry off (with "away")
26 Be suitable for
27 Speak your mind

28 What a storm does
29 Little bit
30 Terrible
31 Monumental gateway
33 "Born, not of ___...but of God" (John 1:13)
34 Meteorologist's tool
35 Nail filing board
36 Ace
39 One of three on Calvary
40 "Wonderful!"
42 Salt addition
43 They "left their __, and followed him" (Matt. 4:20)

46 Jesus rode into Jerusalem on one
48 __ -garde
49 Certain choir member
50 Belly feature
51 Makes fair
52 Brief
54 First man
56 Jesus healed many who were this
57 Former fast flier
58 What they did at the Last Supper
59 2,000 pounds
61 Pie __ mode (2 words)

HE WALKED AMONG US

ACROSS

1 Miracles, e.g.
6 Declare
10 Outlaw
13 "Blessed is the man to whom the Lord will not __ sin" (Rom. 4:8)
15 Key __ pie
16 Chemical suffix
17 Treasurer
18 Jesus, __ of Bethlehem
19 Elizabeth bore a son in her old __
20 Jesus saves His people from their __
22 Jesus, God's __ Son
24 Shape
26 John the Baptizer's "meat was locusts and __ honey" (Matt. 3:4)
28 Vale
29 "The tongue can no man __" (James 3:8)
30 "__ unto me...I will give you rest" (Matt. 11:28)
31 "Last error shall be __ than the first" (Matt. 27:64)
32 Spanish Mrs. (Abbr.)
33 Over 50 group (Abbr.)
34 Mary brought forth __ first born Son
35 Egypt tourist destination
37 Main mast
41 "I will not with ink and __ write unto thee" (3 John 1:13)
42 Jesus washed His disciples'
43 Undergarment

44 Not one mile, but "go with him __" (Matt. 5:41)
47 New Testament book
48 "When ye see the south wind __" (Luke 12:55)
49 Sins
50 Former Russian ruler
51 Small bird
52 Archangel name
54 Paul's missionary destination
56 School group (Abbr.)
57 "They __ nigh unto Jerusalem" (Matt. 21:1)
59 Like Herod's palace, e.g.
63 "Then was Jesus __ up of the Spirit" (Matt. 4:1)
64 "News about him spread throughout the surrounding __" (Luke 4:37 NIV)
65 Bee's interest
66 "Come down __ my child die" (John 4:49)
67 Bible appendix, often
68 Queen of __, Solomon's visitor

DOWN

1 Lie
2 Flightless bird
3 Easter month, often (Abbr.)
4 Row
5 Stodgy
6 Clerical garment
7 Doable
8 Implant
9 Pull in a fish
10 Dam-building animal
11 Attendants at Jesus' birth
12 Can a camel go through its eye?

Across

14 Gray sea eagle
21 Peter's weapon at Jesus' arrest
23 Smells
24 Jesus' mom
25 Delaware town
27 Rascal
29 Recipe measure (Abbr.)
30 Eve's son
31 Jesus did this at Lazarus's tomb
33 Last word in prayer
34 Garden tools
36 Imitative
37 Neon fish
38 "Are ye __ to drink of the cup?" (Matt. 20:22)
39 Press
40 "Which is the great commandment in the __?" (Matt. 22:36)
42 Gov. lending agency (Abbr.)
44 Jesus' place of worship
45 Matthew or Luke, e.g.
46 44 Down had one
47 Jesus' disciples in Garden of Gethsemane
48 He is the vine, you are the __
50 __ cotta
51 Electrical connections
53 Eden male
55 Jesus, God's __
58 Mary __ espoused to Joseph
60 What they did at the Last Supper
61 Check
62 New Testament __

14

GIFTS OF THE SPIRIT

ACROSS

1 "Power of Christ may __ upon me" (2 Cor. 12:9)
5 Prominent fellow
10 Vane dir. (Abbr.)
13 Dole out
15 Where many martyrs died
16 Haw's partner
17 It justifies believers
18 Swine "ran violently down a __ place into the sea" (Mark 5:13)
19 Jesus began His ministry at about 30 years of __
20 Explosive (Abbr.)
21 "Envy __ the bones" (Prov. 14:30 NIV)
23 Creatures "hath been __ of mankind" (James 3:7)
25 We are "baptized into one __" (1 Cor. 12:13)
26 Holy threesome
28 Holy Spirit "__ you by our gospel" (2 Thess. 2:14)
31 KJV Spirit
32 Columbia, Cornell and Dartmouth, for short
33 Pack of paper
34 Curtsy
37 Health food store staple
38 Wishy-washy
40 Former Italian currency
41 Poor man had "one little __ lamb" (2 Sam. 12:3)
42 Voting group
43 Hand lotion brand
44 Fruit of the Spirit
45 Spirit-given insight
46 Classic TV detective

49 "I __ up by revelation" (Gal. 2:2)
50 Paris bye
51 "If ye __ and devour one another" (Gal. 5:15)
52 Airport info (Abbr.)
55 French possessive
56 Converted by the Spirit
59 "Blessed are they that __" (Matt. 5:4)
61 Before (poet.)
62 Have being
63 Moses' brother
64 Hallucinogenic drug (Abbr.)
65 Spiritual result of disbelief
66 Mariana "Peaceful Island"

DOWN

1 Huckleberry Finn's ride
2 Dash
3 Needle's eye, for one
4 Little one
5 Abhorrent to the Spirit
6 Satanic __, forbidden by the Spirit
7 Garden buzzer
8 Three Persons, __ God
9 Sacrament
10 Indian lamb kebab
11 Sire
12 Like a field sown with sin, according to parable,
14 "I'm in the __ of death" (2 Sam. 1:9 NIV)
22 Strange
24 "Go to the __, thou sluggard" (Prov. 6:6)
25 Sky shade (Fr.)

26 "If children, __ heirs"
   (Rom. 8:17)
27 Spirit keeps you on the right one
28 Refer to
29 Declare
30 Spirit's gift to you
31 God's mercy
34 Holy Spirit symbol
35 Don't fiddle with its middle
36 Is there none in Gilead?
38 Yap
39 Insane (Sp.)
40 Spirit's no-no
42 Bewildered
43 Movie theater
44 Poet Edgar Allen

45 Like the Sea of Galilee
46 Sinai sight
47 Bad smells
48 Wrinkled
49 Measurement for Noah's ark
51 "Covet earnestly the __ gifts"
   (1 Cor. 12:31)
52 Vacation money, perhaps
53 Horse's gait
54 Spirit-filled temple prophetess
57 "The __ is laid unto the root
   of the trees" (Luke 3:9)
58 Through
60 Peter's need

15

APOSTLES

ACROSS

1 "If we __ to commune with thee, wilt thou be grieved?" (Job 4:2)
6 Apostle James's brother
10 Piercing pain
14 Most populous country
15 Capital of Western Samoa
16 Martha's worry at Lazarus's tomb
17 Apostles laid on __ to heal the sick
18 Fido, maybe
19 Oompah-pah instrument
20 Big jug
21 Glitch (2 words)
23 Time measure (Abbr.)
24 OT and NT periods, e.g.
26 Maybe Baby Jesus had one
28 Apostolic Christianity (2 words)
31 Simon or Andrew, e.g.
32 Apostles cast __ demons
33 What Apostles preached
36 "__ us not into temptation"
40 African antelopes
42 End Times event
43 Apostle Matthew's Hebrew name
44 Apostle Paul's mission territory
45 Apostles' shoe
48 Lower limb
49 Let not "that day come __ you unawares" (Luke 21:34)
51 Two or more men (Abbr.)
53 Apostle who introduced Nathanael to Jesus
56 Give up
57 "Behold the fowls of the __" (Matt. 6:26)
58 Like the wooden horse
61 Invitation letters (Abbr.)

65 Needs for snowy slopes
67 Nerve fiber
68 Benefit
69 Personal hardship, sometimes
70 Apostles made distribution according to __
71 Slow, in music
72 Sodom after brimstone fell
73 Jesus, God's __ Son
74 Apostles continued in the breaking of __

DOWN

1 Be in pain
2 Playwright George Bernard
3 Trigonometric function
4 Apostle Peter's brother
5 Casual affirmations
6 Apostle son of Alphaeus
7 Musical composition
8 Website visits
9 __ body, opposed to spiritual body
10 Golden item in ark of the covenant
11 Scorched
12 Peace Prize
13 Apostolic gift
21 BLT condiment, informally
22 Cooking spray
25 Tabloid, slangily
27 "Whether in the body, I cannot __" (2 Cor. 12:2)
28 Roman garment
29 Central Asian nomadic herdsmen
30 Decorative needle case
31 Computer expert, maybe

34 Elegant bird
35 Pot's pal
37 Snaky fish
38 Maintain
39 Dwelling, informally
41 Apostle Paul's former name
45 Church choir section
46 "It shall be so" in prayer
47 "He was __ as a sheep to the slaughter" (Acts 8:32)
50 Hell, described as a bottomless __
52 What an elder is meant to be
53 Italian meal staple
54 Climbs
55 Like 2 Down
56 Something for a sweet tooth
59 Animals sold in the temple
60 OT Bible book

62 Lucid
63 Brief autobiographical sketch
64 Proceed sluggishly
66 Swine's house
68 Clerical garment

NEW TESTAMENT BOOKS

ACROSS

1 Zebedee to John, informally
4 Luncheon salad
9 Church server
14 "I took the little book...and __ it up" (Rev. 10:10)
15 Parasite
16 "Whosoever shall not receive you...__ off the dust of your feet" (Matt. 10:14)
17 Yang's partner
18 He wrote two epistles
19 Gave a lavish party
20 Luke's profession
22 Crete, for one
24 Ephesus locale
25 Kid
27 Moralistic
31 Cheerleader's cry
32 Insane
33 Poetic contraction
34 There are "many __ of voices in the world" (1 Cor. 14:10)
36 Jacket filler
38 Evening party
40 Ropes
42 Book after Hebrews
43 Better
44 "__ Maria"
45 Make one
47 Winged
51 "Let us not __ it, but cast lots" (John 19:24)
53 The widow's __
54 Continental currency
55 __ Minor (Little Dipper)
57 Dar es __, Tanzania
59 Riser (arch.)

62 Square
65 Sports org. (Abbr.)
66 Woolen
67 Unresponsive
68 Ado
69 Shapes
70 Short epistles, maybe
71 Medical research org. (Abbr.)

DOWN

1 Peanut caramel bar
2 Impractical
3 Epistle writer's need
4 Fido's feast
5 Witch of Endor, e.g.
6 Stroke
7 Summer tea need
8 Gospel subject
9 Former athletic assoc. (Abbr.)
10 Psalm 23 grazers
11 Former Sunday accessory
12 Make do
13 "By faith they passed through the __ sea" (Heb. 11:29)
21 Early movie innovation
23 Where Prodigal Son worked
25 Book before Revelation
26 UFO riders
28 Fix again
29 Annoys
30 Mediterranean, e.g. (Fr.)
32 Corinth to Philippi (dir.)
35 Tax agency
36 Belonging to (Suffix)
37 Holy Land
38 What 8 Down came to do
39 5 Down might detect one
40 Everlasting __

(Crossword grid)

41 "If __ man thirst, let him come" (John 7:37)
42 Wedding at Cana need
43 Those who look back are not "__ for the kingdom of God" (Luke 9:62)
45 Conversation fillers
46 B vitamin
48 Angolan capital
49 Semitic language
50 Paul's theological treatise
52 Fooled
56 Warm color groups
57 Beget
58 Longest NT book
59 Religious scholar's deg. (Abbr.)
60 Number of epistles to Timothy
61 Moray
63 Card game

64 Wager

17

GOD'S PROMISES

ACROSS

1 Sicilian volcano
5 Paul's travels, often (2 words)
10 Wheel's tooth
13 Book holder
15 Musician/poet Leonard
16 Tokyo tie
17 God promises you this to do great things
18 Foot parts
19 Sports figure, for short
20 Holy Land edible
21 "John and...Pharisees __ to fast" (Mark 2:18)
23 "Every day they __ my words" (Ps. 56:5)
25 At Jesus' trial, a soldier __ Him
26 "Hast thou not poured me out... and curdled me like __?" (Job 10:10)
28 God promises you this as you walk His way
31 Hymn sound
32 Mirror shapes, often
33 Intones a rhyming patter, e.g.
34 Make taboo
37 Frolic
38 Gain a point
40 God promises you this always
41 Psalm 23 creature
42 Sin, e.g.
43 Author Carroll
44 God promises comfort when you do this
45 Sinner __ to temptation
46 Princess dress, e.g.
49 King David's dad, familiarly
50 Repeal

51 God promises you this when you're burdened
52 Offense against God
55 River (Sp.)
56 Crete and Cyprus, e.g.
59 Bring joy
61 Put treasures "where neither moth __ rust doth corrupt" (Matt. 6:20)
62 God promises to provide these
63 God promises to __ leave you
64 GPS letters
65 They come in gaggles
66 New product ad, perhaps

DOWN

1 Sports channel
2 pronoun
3 Salamander
4 Brew
5 God's comfort soothes these
6 Has digits
7 Mary or Martha, e.g.
8 Conger
9 God promises these when you pray
10 Apples have them
11 Extremely heavy
12 Spirit's favors
14 "Bring forth...__ worthy of repentance" (Luke 3:8)
22 Pigpen
24 "Behold a great __ dragon" (Rev. 12:3)
25 God's assistance
26 What fire and brimstone do
27 We have this for the future
28 Lazarus's affliction

29 Declare
30 Jesus' "__ spread abroad" (Mark 1:28)
31 Heavenly promise
34 One of seven poured out in Revelation
35 Passionate
36 Loch __ monster
38 Ghetto
39 God promises that He will __ about you
40 Dregs
42 Hitting player while they're shooting
43 God promises to do this when you pray
44 Computer data handler (Abbr.)
45 Amen!
46 Chili con __

47 Hamburger enhancement, maybe
48 Sleep sound
49 Jesus, Root of __
51 Color wheel section
52 God promises to __ those who believe
53 Detail
54 Roman persecutor of Christians
57 God promises to __ you wherever you are
58 Downwind
60 "They had bound him, they __ him away" (Matt. 27:2)

GOD'S GOOD SERVANTS

ACROSS

1 "Ye shall not eat of them that __ the cud" (Deut. 14:7)
5 Commercials
8 Fluffy's feet
12 Grocery section
13 Be "swift to hear, slow to __" (James 1:19)
15 Healing plant
16 High
17 Artist Matisse
18 Cast "all your __ upon him (1 Peter 5:7)
19 Boston team
21 "Consider carefully what you __ to do" (Acts 5:35 NIV)
23 He questioned why Jesus would 56 Down and 45 Across
25 Pain measure (Abbr.)
26 Kind of knife
29 Jesus, God's __
31 "Can papyrus grow...where there is no __?" (Job 8:11 NIV)
35 Riddle
37 Three persons, __ God
39 Cocoon dweller
40 Seer's claim (Abbr.)
41 Wave riding
44 Weekday (Abbr.)
45 With 56 Down, how Jesus would serve in Upper Room
47 Bowels
48 "Eschew evil, and __" (1 Peter 3:11) (2 words)
50 Play a guitar
52 Land east of Eden
54 "Faith, if it hath not __, is dead" (James 2:17)

55 Vane dir. (Abbr.)
57 Jesus healed many at the __ of death
59 Breath mint
62 Left over, like merchandise
65 Pocket bread
66 Crept, as Judas from Upper Room
68 Flow out slowly
70 "Mine eyes have __ thy salvation" (Luke 2:30)
71 Weighty
72 Urn
73 Salvation __
74 Court
75 Swirl

DOWN

1 Des Moines summer hour
2 He that has ears to __
3 Women's magazine
4 Boar (2 words)
5 Summits
6 "Ye have made it a __ of thieves" (Luke 19:46)
7 Indian garment
8 Car race start (2 words)
9 Actor Alda
10 "Ye heard the __ of truth" (Eph. 1:13)
11 "__ then that ye walk circumspectly" (Eph. 5:15)
13 Ruined
14 Good Servant is this to others
20 Appears to be
22 Resurrection doubter, familiarly
24 House cover
26 Gripes

27 Genesis
28 Duster
30 "Nothing more to add" (Abbr.)
32 Good servant wouldn't spread one
33 Frighten
34 Good servant's natural tools
36 Summer mo. (Abbr.)
38 Omega
42 "I have not __ in vain" (Phil. 2:16)
43 Choir robes
46 Italian region
49 Good servants do this for the lonely (3 wds.)
51 Denver winter hour (Abbr.)
53 "__ others" (2 words)
56 See 45 Across

58 Fingers after writing an epistle, maybe
59 Level
60 Detail
61 Ball of yarn
63 Good servant shuns __ behavior
64 Good servant does a good one
65 Helpful broadcast (Abbr.)
67 ET's ride
69 Snoop

CHRISTIAN LIFE

ACROSS

1 People salute them
6 Slumps
10 Christian __ of heaven
14 Juliet's love
15 Christians __ others
16 Be "perfect, __ as your Father...is perfect" (Matt. 5:48)
17 Where grasses of fields go, according to Jesus
18 What lion-like adversary does, according to Peter
19 Sea of Galilee transport
20 Lady's man, for short
21 Sabbath Day
23 Winter hazard
24 "I Am Jesus' Little __"
26 Metal joiner
28 Lesotho capital
31 Choir section
32 Joppa to Jerusalem (dir.)
33 Herons
36 Dog's breakfast, maybe
40 Former New York stadium
42 Bishop must be "__ to teach" (1 Tim. 3:2)
43 Steadfast, as in faith
44 Sabbath song
45 Christian talk with God
48 Old evil __
49 Christian should not tell one
51 High church service, often
53 __ song, contemporary worship music
56 Fencing sword
57 Desire, with "for"
58 Played (2 words)
61 Tap in lightly

65 Drags
67 Christian cares for body and __
68 First name in cosmetics
69 Nobel Prize city
70 "Repent; or __ I will come" (Rev. 2:16)
71 Marketplace where Paul spoke
72 Christian might ask God for this
73 hart
74 Lassos

DOWN

1 Plague pest
2 What fills Christian's heart
3 Final word for 45 Across
4 Ideal Christian words and actions
5 Steelwool soap pad brand
6 Banished Hagar laid her child under one
7 Billions of years
8 Rejoice and be __
9 Spreads out
10 NT book after Philem. (Abbr.)
11 Elliptic
12 "__ be with you"
13 "__ not into temptation" (Matt. 26:41)
21 Christian should not be this
22 Peter drew in great catch, "__ was not the net broken" (John 21:11)
25 KJV art
27 While away the time
28 Web
29 Sodom after fire and brimstone fell

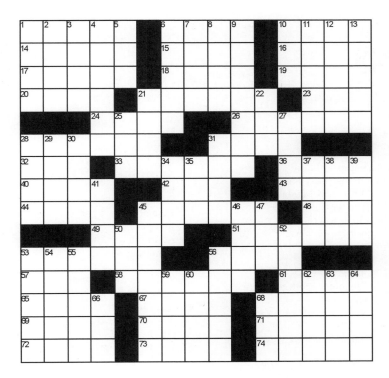

30 "If any man __ to be contentious" (1 Cor. 11:16)
31 Court counselor (Abbr.)
34 "Lips that speak knowledge are a __ jewel" (Prov. 20:15 NIV)
35 Climate watchdog group (Abbr.)
37 Christian's have eternal __
38 Teen dance event
39 Bad one means trouble ahead
41 Against (Prefix)
45 "My beloved Son, in whom I am well __" (Matt. 3:17)
46 Sports channel
47 antelope
50 17 Across remains
52 Christian __ of bitterness (2 words)
53 Tall post
54 Recyclers do this

55 Point of view
56 Swiss mathematician
59 Portion, with "out"
60 Christian should not have a short one
62 At the peak of
63 Christians know they are a __ human
64 Green legumes
66 Lawn
68 "First the blade, then the __" (Mark 4:28)

FIRST CHRISTMAS

ACROSS

1 Bug spray brand
5 Opposed to (dial.)
9 "Be __ with sandals" (Mark 6:9)
13 Teen woe
14 Christmas carol has one
15 Jesus' tomb closure
16 Make calm, as Mary might her Baby
17 Prong
18 "He that reapeth receiveth __" (John 4:36)
19 What heavenly host sang
21 Pull along
23 Manger mattress, according to song
24 Bethlehem to Jericho (dir.)
25 First Christmas singers
29 Joseph to Jesus, humanly speaking
30 Good fortune
32 Pie __ mode (2 words)
33 Ride for 36 Down
36 Saunter
37 Auto fuel
38 Not many (2 words)
39 What Jesus does
40 Temple priest's robe adornments
41 Store treasures that will not do this
42 __ of Scripture, where His Word is found
43 Tropical eel
44 36 Down gold, e.g.
45 Same cite as previous (Latin)
46 At Christmas, be glad, not __!

47 Tax collector Matthew may have kept one
49 Easter mo., often (Abbr.)
50 Kansas City hour at Christmas (Abbr.)
53 Summer tea choice
55 King of kings, e.g.
57 Blooper
60 Asian ruler
62 Fisherman's need
63 Revises
64 36 Down origin, with "the"
65 Holy Child, e.g.
66 Jesus and playmates, once
67 "Lions roar after their __" (Ps. 104.21)
68 What 36 Down saw

DOWN

1 Honeymooner's fellow
2 Sporty car brand
3 Decorative design, sometimes
4 Cafe'
5 Christians __ church on Christmas
6 Christ came in the __ of a little child
7 There was no room for them there
8 God knows your every one
9 Canned chili brand
10 One fed by Prodigal Son
11 "Voice of __ crying in the wilderness" (Matt. 3:3)
12 __ Moines
15 Deluxe
20 Make airtight

22 Speed contests
26 Kids are this on Christmas morning
27 33 Across relative
28 Mouthy
29 When this settled, manna appeared
30 "God so __ the world"
31 Wields
33 Christmas song
34 Christ was "promised __ by his prophets" (Rom. 1:2)
35 God "__ out heaven with the span" (Isa. 40:12)
36 Travelers to Bethlehem
39 Blade
40 Jesus, fully human and fully __
42 Parts
43 Jesus' mom

46 Fancy
48 36 Down brought some
49 "__, and take the young child and his mother" (Matt. 2:13)
50 Sports shoe feature
51 Stone
52 Mary __ Moore
54 "Who shall descend into the __?" (Rom. 10:7)
56 Swords of the Spirit, e.g.
57 "__ thee hence, Satan" (Matt. 4:10)
58 Hubbub, as on Christmas morning
59 Jesus makes us __ to serve others
61 Scratch

BY THE NUMBERS-NEW TESTAMENT

ACROSS

1 One-celled organism
6 Former JFK lander
9 Biblical anointing liquids
13 Fragrant bush
14 "Consider the lilies...__ they grow" (Matt. 6:28)
15 Beginning
16 's big crowd
17 Deli sandwich choice
18 What broke out when Paul preached, often
19 hast
20 Gradation
22 Bible snake
23 Birthday number
24 John Hancock, for short
25 Caesar's garment
27 Put in motion
29 Tehran resident
33 Scandinavian carrier
34 Parable of the __ virgins
35 What tithers do
36 Shroud city
39 Family member, for short
40 Impose
41 At no time "__ we flattering words" (1 Thess. 2:5)
42 Southwestern Indian
43 Christmas tree, often
44 Forgive others __ times seven
46 Egg shape
49 One of seven opened in Revelation
50 Who shall "give them their... meat in __ season?" (Luke 12:42)
51 Shakespearean prince
53 Bible times metal
56 Godly person isn't one
58 Abraham to Isaac, e.g.
59 Paradise, e.g.
61 Clock measure (Abbr.)
62 Artery
63 Days and nights Jesus fasted
64 Jesus fed a crowd with __ fishes
65 One is narrow and one is broad
66 Ice sheet
67 Prodigal Son's home for a spell
68 David and Bathsheba's meeting at first

DOWN

1 With 15 down, first and last
2 Sinai Desert sight, perhaps
3 Faith chapter: Hebrews __
4 "__ things of the world...are despised" (1 Cor. 1:28)
5 House coolers (Abbr.)
6 Unbelieving response to Gospel message
7 Nutritious Asian plant
8 Sem. students' age range, usually
9 God's __ and only Son
10 Crete, e.g. (Sp.)
11 Sediments
12 "Let us keep in __ with the Spirit" (Gal. 5:25 NIV)
15 See 1 Down
20 Plague lice
21 "Except a __ of wheat fall into the ground" (John 12:24)
24 Copier function
26 Some sweaters
28 Stage whispers
30 Crosses on Calvary, Roman style

31 Eleventh month of Jewish calendar
32 Peter, James, and John's need
34 "Bind them...upon thine heart, and __ them about thy neck" (Prov. 6:21)
36 Arizona airport (Abbr.)
37 "Pray for them which despitefully __ you" (Luke 6:28)
38 Preacher, for short
39 Salon employees
40 Jesus fed a crowd with __ loaves
42 Beehive State
43 Number of Gospels
45 Recently
47 Number of Judas's pieces of silver
48 Worlds
50 Hunter's accessory

52 "He that is __ among you... shall be great" (Luke 9:48)
53 What arose between Mary and Martha once
54 Baal
55 Christian persecutor
57 Salamander
58 You might do this on eagle's wings
60 What they did at the Last Supper
62 38 Down must be __ to teach

CHRISTIAN'S LIFE CHALLENGES

ACROSS

1 "People sat down to eat and drink, and rose up to __" (1 Cor. 10:7)
5 Severs
9 "From the __ of the foot...unto the head" (Isa. 1:6)
13 One without trials, e.g.
14 Leave out, as bad behavior
15 Ill-advised antic
16 Materialism, e.g.
17 Respond to God's will this way
18 Swimming mammal
19 Hopelessness, a challenge
21 Be jealous, a challenge
23 Chemical ending (Suffix)
24 Genetic data carrier (Abbr.)
25 Airborne
29 Jesus' was not broken by Roman soldiers
30 Do not "fulfill the __ of the flesh" (Gal. 5:16)
32 Keats composition
33 Tempter
36 Impressionist painter
37 Faucet
38 Promote
39 Subdue, as temptation
40 Anger, a challenge
41 "Put off...the __ man, which is corrupt" (Eph. 4:22)
42 Twilight
43 Stun gun
44 Also
45 "Whoever __ this bread will live" (John 6:51 NIV)
46 Spiritual gift

47 Result of chronic challenge, often
49 Snare
50 Tam
53 Caesar's eight
55 Shelters
57 Cutting beam
60 Stumble, as into sin
62 God the Father
63 Church feature
64 God's consolation
65 Do according to God's __
66 "Let him __ himself, and take up his cross" (Mark 8:34)
67 Jar
68 Fisherman's boat part

DOWN

1 Self-love, a challenge
2 Burdened, as with worry
3 "Sea __ by reason of a great wind" (John 6:18)
4 Bark in pain
5 Baby Jesus is doing this, maybe
6 Dark shadow
7 Bind
8 Eye infection
9 Mythological woodland creature
10 Choose, as good over evil
11 Downwind
12 Sin
15 Wants another's stuff, a challenge
20 Yemeni Gulf of __
22 Of the nose
26 Itty-bitty bits
27 One of many in Proverbs
28 Biblical outcast

29 Fall behind
30 Stew veggies
31 What sin looks like, e.g.
33 "__ they are and blemishes"
   (2 Peter 2:13)
34 Distribute
35 English royal name
36 "They shook off the __ of their
   feet against them" (Acts 13:51)
39 Pseudo
40 Sunbeam
42 Unhindered wants, a challenge
43 Cheap cigar (slang)
46 Biblical precious gem
48 "__ one that asketh receiveth"
   (Matt. 7:8)
49 Overly innocent
50 Biblical measurement
51 Wander

52 Sacred poem
54 Crete or Cyprus
56 Ten Commandments, e.g.
57 Acid drug
58 Mimic worldly people, a
   challenge
59 Do wrong, a challenge
61 "Brother of __ degree rejoice" (James 1:9)

23

GOD'S WILL

ACROSS

1 Carpet choice
5 Former Russian ruler
9 Psalm, e.g.
13 "Moses made a serpent...put it upon a __" (Num. 21:9)
14 Bruin's home
15 God's will: not your weakness, but His __
16 Knows about (2 words)
17 Campus mil. unit (Abbr.)
18 What steeple bell does
19 God's will: be __ with what you have
21 Style
23 Work unit
24 Former military, for short
25 Not two masters, "for __ he will hate the one..." (Matt. 6:24)
29 God's will: bring this to those who need help
30 Cloaks and togas, e.g.
32 KJV's art
33 "__ to the glory of God" (1 Cor. 10:31) (2 words)
36 Mealtime no-no
37 Israelite tribe
38 God's will: be a __ steward
39 Mention certain authorities
40 Foolish remark, sometimes
41 __ Baba
42 God's will: be harmless as __
43 Gardeners' needs
44 Bible land sea
45 Detail
46 God's will: be courageous, not __

47 One most liberated from sin, e.g.
49 Angel's halo, for one
50 Jesus ascended and __ at God's right hand
53 Campus locale, for short
55 Portliness
57 God's Son
60 Humorist Bombeck
62 "Rejoice...__ for joy" (Luke 6:23)
63 Eagle's nest
64 Crucifixion need
65 Gawk
66 Stumble, as into sin
67 Community org. (Abbr.)
68 Wickedness, in parables

DOWN

1 Myrrh
2 God's will: __ parents
3 God's will: get __ with others
4 Fellow, for short
5 "Ye __ to God from idols" (1 Thess. 1:9)
6 Composer Francis __ Key
7 Keyboard key
8 God's will: run the __ set before you
9 God's will: __ others toward Him
10 God's will: cast the beam out of your __ eye
11 Brainwave meas. (Abbr.)
12 Priscilla to Aquila, today
15 God's will: __ Him with songs of thanksgiving
20 God's will: avoid this!
22 Hosiery choice
26 Hell

27 God's forgiveness will __ guilt
28 Tears, style
29 Brew
30 OT idolatrous emblem
31 Miners' quests
33 Snow White friend
34 Tanker
35 God's will: do not lay __ His commandments
36 God's will: __ cheerfully
39 Terra __, patio decor
40 God's will: let Him fill your heart with __
42 Neglect
43 God's will: have __ for the future
46 Secret rabbinical doctrines
48 God's Spirit will __ you to do His will

49 Very funny
50 "Set thy face toward the __ of Jerusalem" (Ezek. 4:7)
51 Dickens's "__ of Two Cities" (2 words)
52 Used a keyboard
54 God's will: __ yourself
56 God's will: be __ to speak
57 James (Abbr.)
58 Conger
59 __ Lanka
61 Uncooked

HEAVENLY HOME

ACROSS

1 KJV's "it came to __"
5 Prophet's pronouncement
10 Los Angeles winter hour
13 Improvise (2 words)
15 Arctic dwelling, maybe
16 One of God's flock, figuratively
17 Heaven is where "the righteous __ forth as the sun" (Matt. 13:43)
18 Intestinal pouch
19 Heaven, where God's __ sits at His right hand
20 Unusual
21 Still sleeping
23 Norwegian inlet
25 Heavenly colors, perhaps
26 "Anyone who __ to do the will of God" (John 7:17 NIV)
28 Heavenly banquet liking
31 Wing-shaped
32 Heavenly vessels made of this
33 __ away from evil!
34 Another name for Lydda, Israel
37 In heaven, there is eternal __
38 Dwelling in heaven, perhaps?
40 Roof material for 38 Across, maybe
41 Superlative ending
42 Now we have __ of heaven
43 "All shapes and __"
44 Pearly Gates host
45 Ornate fabric for heavenly banquet?
46 Lessen
49 Brief epistle
50 Singer Ronstadt
51 42 Across is a gift of the __ Spirit
52 Choose
55 __ Times
56 Asian nation
59 In heaven there's a __ of life
61 "They would have repented long __" (Matt. 11:21)
62 Colder
63 You might do this upon entering heaven!
64 Heaven, the __ Jerusalem
65 Sequence
66 Swerve

DOWN

1 El __, Texas
2 Widespread childhood condition (Abbr.)
3 Skidded
4 Christ came to take away the guilt of __
5 We won't have these in heaven
6 Like Anna in the Temple
7 What the Comforter gives (Abbr.)
8 Wasteful steward of parable had a large one (Abbr.)
9 Promise of heaven gives us __
10 Spanish currency
11 Peter did this when he denied Jesus
12 Inclines
14 It will surround you in heaven
22 It won't sting you in heaven
24 Permanent heavenly state
25 Peter Cottontail, for one
26 Chunk
27 Maybe you'll wear on in heaven
28 Mound

29 Car rental agency
30 Attic
31 Lil' comic strip fellow
34 Ms. Minnelli
35 Spain stadium cheers
36 Writing need
38 __ d'Ivoire, Africa
39 Heaven's gates swing __
40 "The __ is at hand" (Rev. 1:3)
42 Dose that acts on the liver
43 Forest sprites of myth
44 Exercise mat
45 Pain unit
46 "Clothed in fine linen, white
   and __" (Rev. 19:14)
47 Pearly Gate need
48 Give
49 __ Dame Cathedral, Paris

51 "Thou shalt bruise his __"
   (Gen. 3:15)
52 White House office
53 South American nation
54 "I give to eat of the __ of
   life" (Rev. 2:7)
57 Winter pavement, perhaps
58 Pen brand
60 "His face was like the sun
   shining in all __ brilliance"
   (Rev. 1:16 NIV)

25

ALL ABOUT PRAYER

ACROSS

1 "Hallowed be thy __"
5 Mimicked
9 In prayer, worries lessen and __
14 Incense producer
15 Choir director's concern
16 Zodiac sign
17 "In thy majesty __ prosperously" (Psa. 45:4)
18 "My __ is exceeding sorrowful" (Matt. 26:38)
19 Monastery figure
20 Ball holder
21 "Come ye...into a desert place, and rest __" (Mark 6:31) (2 words)
23 In Christmas skits, Baby Jesus __ in a manger
24 "__ yourselves in the sight of the Lord" (James 4:10)
26 Compete
28 "__ Father"
29 "Excuse me"
31 "Take your __ and go home" (Matt. 9:6 NIV)
34 Awkwardly
37 Spiritual result of prayer, often
39 Psalmist, for one
40 Financial review sheet letters
41 Twin Cities state (Abbr.)
42 Accumulate
44 God's presence means you'll never be this
47 "If ye be __ of the Spirit" (Gal. 5:18)
48 Kitty-cat
50 Crackpot
51 "Stand in the __" (Ezek. 22:30)
52 Puts up
56 Biblical idol
59 Bun topping seed
63 "Gotcha!"
64 Nettle
66 Cartoon bear
67 Biblical calendar month
68 "Laying up in __ for themselves a good foundation" (1 Tim. 6:19)
69 Great Lake
70 KJV cows
71 African nation
72 They "hid...in the __ and in the rocks" (Rev. 6:15)
73 Brews

DOWN

1 "They shall come from the east... from the __" (Luke 13:29)
2 Bye-bye (Fr.)
3 Desktop need
4 Before (poet.)
5 You pray, God __
6 Winnie-the-__
7 Decorative needle case
8 Glade
9 Chicken __ king (2 words)
10 Where the Lord's Prayer is found
11 What you may call God
12 Helen of __
13 Jesus __ with sinners
21 College grad, for short
22 First lady
25 Spells
27 Mischievous tot
29 Some choir members

1	2	3	4	■	5	6	7	8	■	9	10	11	12	13

(crossword grid)

30 Sunday song
31 Injure seriously
32 Facial blemish
33 __ Commandments
34 "__ unto me...and I will give you rest" (Matt. 11:28)
35 "__ us not into temptation"
36 We may ask God to heal ours
38 Express feelings
39 Buddy
43 Resting place
45 Pray for your __
46 Be __ that God will answer your prayers
49 Package deliverer (Abbr.)
51 With 54 Down: "For __ is the kingdom, and the __" (Matt. 6:13)
53 Carp

54 See 51 Down
55 Jesus __
56 Lie in the sun
57 Stake
58 Later
60 Ogled
61 Tender
62 Opposed to (dial.)
65 "__ rather, blessed are they that hear the word of God" (Luke 11:28)
67 Paul __ Saul (Abbr.)

NEW TESTAMENT EVENTS

ACROSS

1 Wind dir. (Abbr.)
5 Roman coliseum, for one
10 Weary shoulders might do this
13 Bind, as soldiers did to Jesus (2 words)
15 At about 30, Jesus would __ His ministry
16 Jesus shows us the __ to heaven
17 "He is risen!" announcer
18 Through Jesus, God would __ us
19 Sin
20 "Amen!"
21 __ of the Apostles, Bible book
23 Adult insect
25 Jesus, from David's ___
26 51 Down __ relationships
28 Jesus ascended into these
31 Civil rights org. (Abbr.)
32 What a goose does
33 "That hurts!"
34 Satan, the old evil __
37 She (Fr.)
38 Church feature
40 Cocoon dweller
41 What angels do
42 "Ye shall in no __ enter into the kingdom" (Matt. 5:20)
43 Apostle in Jerusalem church
44 "God so loved the __"
45 Museum guide
46 Greek muse of music
49 "When ye __, be not...of a sad countenance" (Matt. 6:16)
50 Cover story
51 Spirit's gift
52 Mary or Martha, e.g.
55 Blabbed, texting style

56 Lowest point
59 Jesus, Prince of __
61 Bard's conjunction
62 Ten Commandment no-no
63 Sunday anthems
64 He brought five loaves and two fish
65 Hell
66 Extra-wide shoes

DOWN

1 "__ here and keep watch" (Mark 14:34 NIV)
2 Jesus changed water into it
3 Prays
4 "If any man will __ thee at the law" (Matt. 5:40)
5 Lessen
6 Cincinnati team
7 Pride
8 "__ it in the bud"
9 Believers first called Christians here
10 Jesus's blood was like___ in Gethsemane
11 "This is disgusting!"
12 Greek sandwiches
14 Scottish fabrics
22 Brain and spinal cord (Abbr.)
24 Wipe
25 21 Across writer
26 Paul's former name
27 Spice
28 Gourmet cook
29 Slouch
30 Jesus, God's __ Son
31 Smelled
34 Rant

35 Jesus' tomb was __
36 Bethlehem star locale
38 Seniors' org. (Abbr.)
39 Crete, for one
40 Agreement
42 Early church city
43 Mary's husband
44 Part of www
45 Injured serviceperson's org. (Abbr.)
46 Artist's need
47 Extreme
48 Measured
49 Walled towns
51 "Believing ye might have __" (John 20:31)
52 Esau's quest
53 Teen's woe

54 Mustard seed is "__ than all the seeds" (Mark 4:31)
57 "Gotcha!"
58 Teacher's advanced deg. (Abbr.)
60 "Beam that is in thine own __" (Matt. 7:3)

JESUS CHRIST

ACROSS

1 Make taboo
4 Spirit "__ light on one's inmost being" (Prov. 20:27 NIV)
9 "Blessed __ the poor in spirit" (Matt. 5:3)
12 Some churchgoers, e.g.
14 Disciple
15 "He that ploweth should __ in hope" (1 Cor. 9:10)
16 Bitterness
17 Heavy-set
18 "Or __ believe me for the... works' sake" (John 14:11)
19 Eternity
21 The Lord's __
23 __ Baba
24 Twitch
25 Stolen property
28 Cell card
31 Half (prefix)
34 Dance to music
36 He came to __ for sin
38 John, the voice of __ crying in the wilderness
40 Hairdo
41 He came from David's __ line
43 Bruin's school
44 Length meas. (Abbr.)
45 Guy's partner
46 __, Son, and Holy Spirit
48 Eden name
51 Jesus gave people this (Abbr.)
53 Nifty
54 They are "as the early __ that passeth away" (Hos. 13:3)
56 Keyboard key
58 Graduates

61 Mary "__ the feet of Jesus" (John 12:3)
66 Greek second letter
67 Capital of Senegal
69 Western treaty group (Abbr.)
70 Bible times edible
71 Christ "shall rise the __ day" (Mark 9:31)
72 Flightless birds
73 Bible land tree
74 Jesus laid __ on the sick
75 Apple or peach, maybe

DOWN

1 Jesus, __ of Bethlehem
2 Tel __, Israel
3 Pharaoh's river
4 Thread holder
5 Ego
6 Fencing sword
7 Snub, for short
8 Risen Christ, "firstfruits of them that __" (1 Cor. 15:20)
9 Supportive friend
10 Christ __ Easter morning
11 Pitcher
13 German article
15 Christ, Prince of __
20 Christ's gift bringers
22 Christ came to __ us of guilt
25 Hagia __, former Istanbul cathedral
26 Christ came to save the __
27 "They would have repented long __ in sackcloth" (Matt. 11:21)
29 Song of Solomon, e.g.
30 "Mama __!"
32 Barista specialty

33 Bay
34 Comics sound
35 Work unit
37 Storybook character
39 Christ restored the high priest servant's
42 Horse tidbit
43 Southwestern Indian
47 Against (Prefix)
49 Publicist
50 Peter, James, and John, e.g.
52 Fabrication
55 Temple or ark measurement
57 Christ, Lord of __
58 Christ invites us to call our Father this
59 Dregs
60 Salt Lake state
61 Related

62 Gaza to Joppa (dir.)
63 Pat down lightly
64 Decorative needle case
65 Med measurement
68 Expression of surprise

28

NEW TESTAMENT MIRACLES

ACROSS

1 He was blinded on 5 Across
5 See 1 Across
9 Bottle
13 Forgive and God will __ forgive you
14 Hand lotion ingredient
15 Make into a god
16 Spirit cleanses yours
17 With 48 Down, Cana miracle element
18 Elect
19 Many miracles were this
21 What Ananias sold
23 Hand communication (Abbr.)
24 Commandment number
25 Chemical salt
29 Miraculously, 1 Across could __ again
30 Soldier did this at Jesus
32 "Let your communication be, Yea, yea; __" (Matt. 5:37)
33 Desktop need
36 European river
37 Fragrant biblical resin
38 Choir solo, perhaps
39 "Thy __ hath made thee whole" (Mark 5:34)
40 Manhattan station
41 What Ananias told concerning 21 Across
42 "I set my face like a __" (Isa. 50:7)
43 Miraculously freed from prison with 1 Across
44 Nursery school pupil
45 Peter healed a __ man

46 "I cannot __; to beg I am ashamed" (Luke 16:3)
47 God will __ your prayers
49 Not "one __ or one tittle shall... pass from the law" (Matt. 5:18)
50 __-Lent, liturgical period
53 "He had lifted up __ upon the thick trees" (Psa. 74:5)
55 "Love your __" (Matt. 5:44)
57 Former full planet
60 "With the Lord Begin Thy __," church hymn
62 Where 54 Down shone
63 Sermons should __ to scripture
64 Malaria fever
65 Wager
66 Martha's fear at Lazarus's tomb
67 Optimistic
68 Two aspirin, e.g.

DOWN

1 Former Turkish title
2 Nicodemus "brought a mixture of myrrh and __" (John 19:39)
3 What a miracle isn't
4 Lounge
5 Native American tribe
6 Arrange
7 2,000 pounds
8 "Thou shalt bruise his __" (Gen. 3:15)
9 World (Ger.)
10 Caesar's three
11 Behind
12 Caustic substance
15 Mean
20 Object
22 Imitative

26 One freed Peter from prison
27 Scandinavian hot place
28 Church songs
29 Jesus walked on it
30 Paris river
31 Greens swing
33 Where 1 Across survived a snake bite
34 Constellation
35 Special menus
36 Apostles healed some who were this
39 Panache
40 Demon was sent into one
42 Bendable joint
43 Holy Land, e.g.
46 Jesus rode one into Jerusalem
48 See 17 Across
49 Miracle worker

50 Accompaniment for children's choir
51 "Spirit of glory...__ on you" (1 Peter 4:14 NIV)
52 Cosmetic counter name
54 Miraculous light over Bethlehem
56 Brew
57 For
58 Jesus __ His disciples to truth
59 ET's craft
61 Prophets told long __ Messiah would come

29

PROPHECIES FULFILLED BY JESUS

ACROSS

1 Plan details, for short
6 "Yikes!"
10 Arabic alphabet start
14 Supple
15 He came to __
16 False prophets __ as Messiah
17 Comics orphan
18 "Is a __ between me and death"
   (1 Sam. 20:3 NIV)
19 His __ will have no end
20 Last Supper, e.g.
21 __ relief, sculptural feature
22 He would be __ from death
24 Donkey pull
26 Bethlehem in Jesus' time, e.g.
27 Docked
30 Coffee
31 Annoyed
32 Not one of His __ would be
   broken
33 With Insp., a book section
36 Chili con __
37 Pan go-with
38 "Like as corn is sifted in a __"
   (Amos 9:9)
40 In the manner of (Fr.) (2 words)
41 Twilights (poet.)
43 Land under Ahasuerus's reign
44 Herb Pharisees would tithe
45 His arms would __ 4 Down
46 He would __ into heaven
49 Hourly pay
50 Spirit helps us __ in faith
51 Holy Innocent, e.g.
52 Chestnut horse
56 Riyadh dweller
57 Metric weight unit

59 Church feature
60 Mongolian desert
61 Halo
62 Actor's parts
63 Smithsonian (Abbr.)
64 Ditch (var.)
65 Calvary sight

DOWN

1 Bang
2 Christmas tree
3 Bunsen burner
4 "Suffer little __...to come unto
   me" (Matt. 19:14)
5 He would cause the blind to __
6 Student's paper
7 Pistols (slang)
8 "__ Maria"
9 Corrupt
10 Easter month, often
11 Plague pest
12 Small land mass
13 He would __ the hungry
21 He will judge good and __
23 Gathering
25 He will be our __
26 They will pierce His __
27 Mineral group
28 Jesus' teaching, e.g.
29 Summer veggie
30 We are "__-heirs with Christ"
   (Rom. 8:17)
32 "Fragrant __, the work of a per-
   fumer" (Ex. 30:25 NIV)
33 Start over
34 He would atone for __
35 He would __ His sheep

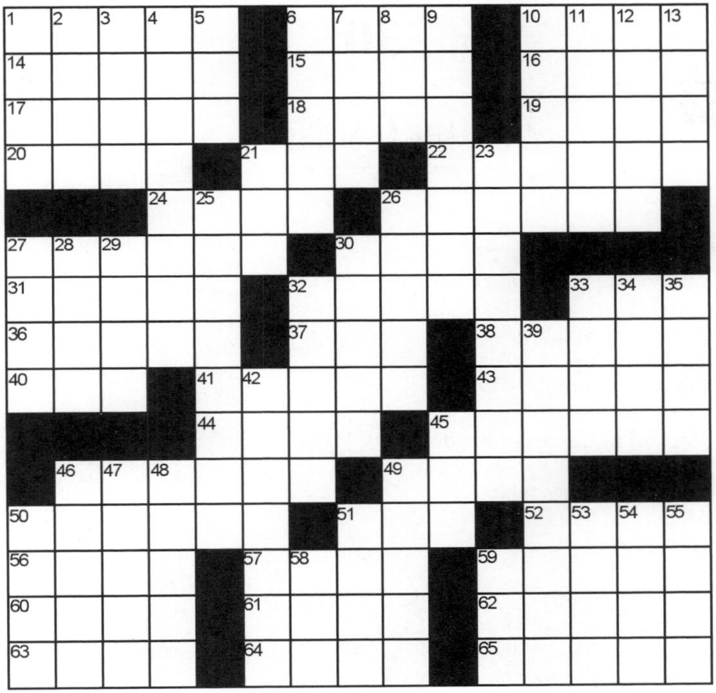

39 "I am not...___ to the 'super-apostles'" (2 Cor. 12:11 NIV)
42 He would be given __ to drink
45 Jesus would __ with sinners
46 Rod of __, tabernacle item
47 Jesus' side piercings, e.g.
48 Biblical measurement
49 He would be born of one
50 They would come to worship Him
51 KJV weed
53 Norwegian city
54 Beers
55 Loch __ monster
58 See 44 across
59 Rainbow shape

30

HOLY SPIRIT

ACROSS

1 "While we __ yet sinners, Christ died" (Rom. 5:8)
5 Pseudo chocolate
10 Toast go-with
13 Japanese poem
15 Sporty car brand
16 Prideful person has a big one
17 Birch-like tree
18 Spirit never does this
19 Mary __ at Jesus' feet
20 Greens need
21 Sky color (Fr.)
23 When "the Spirit of __, is come, he will guide you" (John 16:13)
25 Spirit __ inside the heart
26 Forger might have many
28 God-given gift
31 KJV Spirit
32 Where Spirit lives in you
33 What the sower of parable sowed in
34 Phone greeting, slangily
37 Great Lake
38 Architect Frank __ Wright
40 Sermon delivery, usually
41 Land east of Eden
42 Sullen
43 Pie serving
44 Spirit's compassion
45 When it's hard to pray, Spirit __ for us
46 Funnel-shaped fish
49 Angel's topper
50 Island greeting
51 Central points
52 Legume

55 "Grieve not the holy Spirit of __" (Eph. 4:30)
56 Whining voice type
59 Shy, cheerful or friendly, e.g.
61 Gaza to Bethlehem (dir.)
62 "Who has insulted the Spirit of __?" (Heb. 10:29 NIV)
63 Holy person
64 Devil's color, popularly
65 "Rich he hath sent __ away" (Luke 1:53)
66 "Lions roar after their __" (Ps. 104:21)

DOWN

1 "__ saith the scripture?" (Rom. 4:3)
2 Spiritual comfort, e.g.
3 Do not "delay to offer the first of thy __ fruits" (Ex. 22:29)
4 Make do (with "out")
5 54 Down projects
6 Freedom org. (Abbr.)
7 Herb tithed by Pharisees
8 Lode yield
9 Spirit's water
10 Like a dove, Spirit descended on Him
11 Multicolored rock
12 "Treasures in heaven, where __... do not destroy" (Matt. 6:20 NIV)
14 Straight
22 "__ your light so shine" (Matt. 5:16)
24 OT unclean rodent
25 Like Sinai Desert
26 Sailor's call

27 "Each one should carry their own __" (Gal. 6:5 NIV)
28 "Art thou __ the Son of God?" (Luke 22:70)
29 Aircraft (prefix)
30 "There is __ up for me a crown of righteousness" (2 Tim. 4:8)
31 "Happy are ye; for the spirit of __...resteth upon you" (1 Peter 4:14)
34 Church solo, maybe
35 "Walk honestly...that ye may have __ of nothing" (1 Thess. 4:12)
36 Madrid stadium sounds
38 Apocryphal story, e.g.
39 Ricky's partner on classic TV
40 Sandwich spread
42 Unsettle

43 Leaves, informally
44 Dashboard reading (Abbr.)
45 Joey's home
46 Brew
47 "Neither pray I for these __" (John 17:20)
48 Out-__, old fashioned
49 Perforated
51 Bible truth, e.g.
52 Animal combo for Noah's ark
53 "__ Kleine Nachtmusik" (Ger.)
54 Court figure (Abbr.)
57 "To whom hath the __ of the Lord been revealed?" (John 12:38)
58 Maple provider
60 Music genre

31

JESUS SAVES

ACROSS

1 Complains
6 Jesus says you can call Father this
10 Forbid, as sin
13 "__ hath overwhelmed me" (Ps. 55:5)
15 Scuba diver's find
16 Poetic contraction
17 Do not __ evildoers
18 There won't be one in heaven
19 Communion cup taker's action
20 Grocery section
22 Jesus came according to God's __
24 Sacks
26 Jesus __ on the cross
28 Where God spoke 22 Across
29 Earring need
30 KJV deer
31 "Every day they __ my words" (Ps. 56:5)
32 Anger
33 Lighted sign
34 Spasm
35 Plead
37 Multiple molecule compound
41 "I am like an __ of the desert" (Ps. 102:6)
42 Jesus saves your __ from death
43 See 6 Down
44 Jesus __ our broken relationship with God
47 Lenten practice, for some
48 Cereal aisle find
49 Spice brought to Jesus' tomb
50 What Jesus died for
51 Bible book of Jesus' birth
52 Separation, as from God
54 Pride gives big ones
56 "__ is laid unto the root of the trees" (Luke 3:9)
57 Commits 50 Across
59 Satan was __ from heaven
63 Clock measure, for short
64 Canal
65 Do not __ God's message
66 New Testament period, e.g.
67 __ God's commandments
68 Author Erich

DOWN

1 Repeated, a dance
2 "Thy __ and thy staff…comfort me" (Ps. 23:4)
3 "He hath shewed strength with his __" (Luke 1:51)
4 Jesus is a __ between us and God
5 Lazarus of parable had many
6 43 Across, KJV style
7 Tapped the horn
8 Jesus wore one
9 Big hairdo
10 Jesus stays __ you
11 Gets up
12 Sorrowful sinners do this
14 Christian school subj. (Abbr.)
21 Foolish one
23 We are saved by God's __
24 Jesus was __ in Bethlehem
25 Assist
27 No room for them in the __
29 Commandment no-no
30 Jesus came to __ sin-sickness
31 "Thy __ be done"
33 Good __, the gospel message

34 Flaunt
36 Beverly Hills' Drive
37 Police force
38 Gospel writer
39 Pennsylvania city
40 Roman king (Lat.)
42 __ Francisco
44 Paris wife (Fr.)
45 Medicinal drink
46 Roman Catholic devotion
47 Storm caused __ winds on Sea
   of Galilee
48 One broke out when Paul
   preached
50 Abort a launch
51 __ Armstrong, trumpeter
53 Begin again

55 "__ so loved the world..."
58 Pig place
60 Tower
61 LAX info (Abbr.)
62 Keyboard key

32

SYMBOLS OF THE CHURCH

ACROSS

1 Cheat
5 Treaty
9 Bible legume
13 1813 Battle of Lake _
14 Wing-like
15 "I will __ on you no longer" (Jer. 3:12 NIV)
16 Measuring instrument (var.)
17 Choir piece, maybe
18 Church feature
19 Race-runner, as Christ's church
21 Church __, cemetery site sometimes
23 James or John's need
24 Storm on Galilee call, maybe
25 Martha's worries at Lazarus's tomb
29 Easter month, often (Abbr.)
30 Plague pests
32 "__, Lord: I believe" (John 11:27)
33 Affliction of many Jesus healed
36 Ado
37 Mary "__ at Jesus' feet" (Luke 10:39)
38 Reveal a secret
39 Resign
40 Face a camera, perhaps
41 "He has performed mighty deeds with his __" (Luke 1:51 NIV)
42 What the healed lame man does
43 "No bread, no bag, no money in your __" (Mark 6:8 NIV)
44 Family member, for short
45 Affectations
46 What James and John might do
47 Several gentlemen, for short
49 East of Eden land
50 Delivery service
53 Church song
55 Like ocean bottom
57 Enlarge
60 Church section
62 Currency in Paris or Rome
63 Append
64 "They that __ soft clothing are in kings' houses" (Matt. 11:8)
65 Sound croaky
66 Shirt clasp
67 Church is the "__ of the earth" (Matt. 5:13)
68 "Resist the devil, and he will __ from you" (James 4:7)

DOWN

1 "Eternal life...promised before the world __" (Titus 1:2)
2 Very angry
3 Church, __ in world of darkness
4 Boat element
5 Church pulpit occupier
6 They were brought to Jesus' tomb
7 Nutritionist's concern (Abbr.)
8 Helen of __
9 Church, the __ of Christ
10 Greek mythological figure
11 Punching tool
12 Vane reading (Abbr.)
15 "The __ sows the word" (Mark 4:14 NIV)
20 Catch sight of
22 Tie choice
26 Household cleaner brand

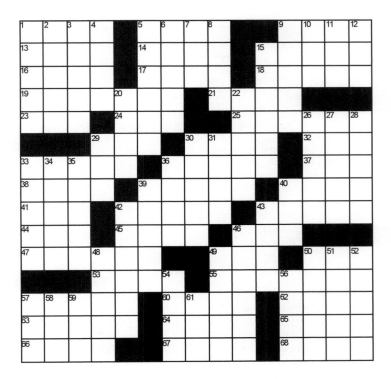

27 Mustard seed "the __ of all seeds" (Matt. 13:32)
28 Fills
29 "__, and it shall be given you" (Luke 11:9)
30 Little leaven leavens many __
31 29 Across bloom, perhaps
33 Blood element
34 Eagle's nest
35 Church is as "__ among wolves" (Luke 10:3)
36 "__ not, little flock" (Luke 12:32)
39 Natural belief in God
40 Church seat
42 Vocal cord locale
43 Church, "the __ of Christ" (1 Cor. 12:27)

46 Former Crystal Cathedral Schuller
48 Christ "giveth his life for the __" (John 10:11)
49 Adenoidal
50 Typical
51 Analyze syntactically
52 Mount of Olives feature, e.g.
54 Negatives, slangily
56 Vassal
57 God is, __, and ever shall be
58 No room for Mary and Joseph here
59 Genetic code (Abbr.)
61 Pot dweller

33

GIFT OF FAITH

ACROSS

1 Faith helps us "__ how wide...deep is" Christ's love (Eph. 3:18 NIV)
6 Spigots
10 Athletic group (Abbr.)
13 Harvest, e.g.
15 "Thy __ be done"
16 Corp. honcho (Abbr.)
17 "__ the sincere milk of the word" (1 Peter 2:2)
18 Black and white snack
19 NT epistle (Abbr.)
20 Orange peel
22 "One Lord, one faith, one __" (Eph. 4:5)
24 __ Reaper, symbol of death
26 Conversion spot for 54 Across
28 Wine skin
29 Judgment __ of Christ
30 Judas would __ himself
31 Frozen pizza brand
32 Lame man's afflicted appendage
33 Faith's gift, __ of heaven
34 Roman Catholic sister
35 Island music maker
37 Ennui
41 Not clerical, in church
42 Times Square feature
43 Pride
44 If salt loses its __, what good is it?
47 Printer ink color
48 Old McDonald had one
49 Serving dish
50 Hockey player's focus
51 Faith's gift, new __ in Christ
52 Flyer's gift, perhaps
54 See 26 Across

56 Tire inflator's concern (Abbr.)
57 "Star Wars" forest creature
59 Winter eave clinger
63 Downwind
64 "__ all that thou hast" (Luke 18:22)
65 Sketch artist
66 Omega
67 Trolley
68 Thrill

DOWN

1 Have faith in __
2 Regret
3 O'Hare people-mover (Abbr.)
4 With 30 Down, faith-giver
5 Jewish festival
6 19 Across epistle number
7 Auto safety device
8 Beg, as for forgiveness
9 Prodigal Son longed to eat some
10 Gift of faith, not just words but __
11 Lively
12 Punctuation marks
14 Commandment number
21 Window treatment
23 Steak
24 Computer expert, slangily
25 Spaghetti sauce choice
27 By faith, we are __ body in Christ
29 Missouri Jesuit school (Abbr.)
30 See 4 Down
31 Convert, e.g.
33 "How shall they __ without a preacher?" (Rom. 10:14)

34 When darkness fell at Jesus'
   crucifixion
36 Architect Frank __ Wright
37 Birds' features
38 Jesus healed many who were __
   and mute
39 Scary creature
40 Mary to Jesus
42 42 Across locale
44 Basic food
45 Christ has __!
46 Diverse, as spiritual gifts
47 Certain church feature
48 Family tie
50 Faith's gift, __ to do right
51 Filthy __, miser's obsession
53 Faith's gift, __ for weary soul
55 Help
58 Dutch airlines

60 EPA legislative concern
   (Abbr.)
61 __ your light shine!
62 Bard's contraction

34

LOVE IS. . .

ACROSS

1 Swing around
5 Fundamental
10 Hebrew letter
13 Winter jacket
15 Methuselah's dad
16 John took the book "and __ it up" (Rev. 10:10)
17 Theme: slow to __
18 Paul's woes, "in danger __" (2 Cor. 11:26 NIV) (2 words)
19 9 Down book (Abbr.)
20 Ball holder
21 Evil in a field, parable-speak
23 Track features
25 Fish hands
26 19 Across, e.g.
28 Last Supper, a spiritual __
31 Theme: not easily brought to this
32 Sever
33 Like an angel, maybe
34 Repeated, word of disapproval
37 __ scallopini, Italian dish
38 Kick out
40 Indonesian island
41 "Tongue is the __ of a ready writer" (Ps. 45:1)
42 Car rental agency
43 Authoritative list, as Bible books
44 "As water ____ on the ground" (2 Sam. 14:14)
45 Garaged the car
46 A __, choir with accompaniment
49 "Like a __ or a sword...is one who gives false witness" (Prov. 25:18 NIV)
50 Egg-shaped
51 Attention-getting calls
52 Before faith, we're under the __
55 Jesus, true God, true __
56 Caffeine pill brand
59 Philippine dish
61 Average
62 Cow's belly
63 Organ setting device
64 Pie __ mode (2 words)
65 Arabian peninsula nation
66 Join together

DOWN

1 Row
2 Path
3 "I __ you to imitate me" (1 Cor. 4:16 NIV)
4 Make do
5 Theme: __ things patiently
6 Wager
7 Distress call
8 Frost
9 Theme, KJV style
10 Implied
11 Coral reef
12 Bible book section
14 Creator
22 "Go to the __, thou sluggard" (Prov. 6:6)
24 Brimstone leaving
25 Theme: It will never __
26 Little Mermaid's love
27 Theme: now we know in __
28 Invitation request (Abbr.)
29 Fencing sword
30 God has a good __ for you
31 Keep belt of truth around your __
34 Chariot descendant, maybe

35 __-eyed, almond shaped feature
36 Theme: is __ to others
38 Theme: thinks no __
39 Bob __, home improvement man
40 Sharp point
42 Theme: joy __ (in abundance)
43 Instrumental
44 "City that is __ on an hill cannot be hid" (Matt. 5:14)
45 Layer
46 Punctuation mark
47 Reward
48 Chinese bamboo eater
49 Cheat
51 Theme: one of three that remain
52 Modern 9 Down
53 First murder victim

54 Theme: gentle in __ and deed
57 Lode yield
58 "Eyes of Israel were __ for age" (Gen. 48:10)
60 Manna came with it

35

SPREAD THE WORD

ACROSS

1 Eden's gardener
5 "He...measured each __ of the porch" (Ezek. 40:48)
9 "He hath __ his bow" (Ps. 7:12)
13 Type choice
14 16 Across missionary companion
15 Church choir voice
16 Called "greatest missionary"
17 Opposed to (dial.)
18 Site of Christian martyrdom
19 Where believers first called Christians
21 Coastal city visited by 16 Across
23 Papua New Guinea city
24 Wager
25 OT prophet
29 "Many as are __ by the Spirit of God" (Rom. 8:14)
30 Sky color (Fr.)
32 Athletic org. (Abbr.)
33 Isaac to Esau: "Prepare me the kind of __ food I like" (Gen. 27:4 NIV)
36 Knobs
37 NYSE heading
38 Joseph's coat was multi-__
39 Extremely zealous
40 Scotland house of worship
41 Psalm, sometimes
42 "Go ye into all the __, and preach" (Mark 16:15)
43 Edibles in Peter's vision (Acts 11:5-7)
44 Pinch
45 Travel on foot
46 Beggar's garb
47 Good News
49 German article
50 Eternity
53 I "am __ than the least of all saints" (Eph. 3:8)
55 Skeptic looks at 47 Across this way
57 Sinners run __ of God's law
60 Modern missionary's transport
62 Fully satisfy
63 45 Across woes
64 Device employer
65 Murdered, slangily
66 45 Across, perhaps
67 "The __ shall be first" (Matt. 20:16)
68 16 Across needed one at times (Abbr.)

DOWN

1 Dismay
2 Ephesians' idol (Acts 19:28)
3 Serious
4 Saharan nation
5 God __ 1 Across in Eden
6 "We __ also to love one another" (1 John 4:11)
7 Slide on snow
8 16 Across knew how to make one
9 16 Across preached here
10 Perga to Derbe (dir.)
11 French negative
12 __-la-la, musical refrain
15 16 Across birthplace
20 Why "ye should not __ the truth?" (Gal. 3:1)

22 "Now __ your members...unto holiness" (Rom. 6:19)
26 Apostle Thomas's mission destination, perhaps
27 Scuttle a shuttle
28 Opposite of doves
29 Company name ender (Abbr.)
30 Where to find 47 Across
31 They __ Jesus in a tomb
33 Sandal part
34 Visual partner
35 Leaks
36 God's word as "a light that shineth in a __ place" (2 Peter 1:19)
39 Churns
40 Container
42 60 Across features

43 John __, traveler with 16 Across
46 Vacation spot
48 Thud
49 Holy Land fruits
50 Authorize
51 Church ensemble, maybe
52 "I am poor and __" (Ps. 40:17)
54 Former name for 16 Across
56 16 Across mission territory
57 She was "taken in adultery, in the very __" (John 8:4)
58 "I thank my God...__ you all" (Rom. 1:8)
59 Lode yield
61 Uncle Sam's land (Abbr.)

36

ALL IN A BIBLE DAY

ACROSS

1 Chew
6 Fine wood
10 Modern-day help for Levi (Mark 2:14) (Abbr.)
13 Cameroon seaport
15 Former Guinean currency
16 Some were masters of decorative __
17 Coiled
18 NT fisherman, for short
19 Fibber's forte
20 Joseph and Zebedee
22 Workbench tool
24 Mary and Joanna
26 Manna measure
28 False front
29 Heaps
30 Hit
31 Book title start, maybe (2 words)
32 Abraham's nephew
33 "Mine eyes have __ thy salvation" (Luke 2:30)
34 Levi's levy
35 Bishop's staff
37 Where chickens gather (2 words)
41 Brain and spinal cord combo (Abbr.)
42 Herod was one
43 Owner of vineyard today, perhaps (Abbr.)
44 Samuel, Gad, and Zadok
47 Saucy
48 "Father knoweth __ things ye have need of" (Matt. 6:8)
49 Writer Bombeck
50 Former Venetian magistrate
51 21 Down need

52 John the Baptizer, for one
54 Input
56 Body design, for short
57 Choir section
59 Uniform
63 Parisian summer (Fr.)
64 Mason's project, maybe
65 Lack of iron
66 Little bit
67 "Mary hath chosen that good __" (Luke 10:42)
68 Complainer

DOWN

1 Omaha summer hour
2 "__ great a matter a little fire kindleth" (James 3:5)
3 French "yes"
4 "Melts in your mouth" candy brand
5 Beggar's cries
6 Kitchen meas.
7 Fancy fabric
8 "I will not...__ what my lips have uttered" (Ps. 89:34 NIV)
9 Ukrainian capital
10 Candle maker's need
11 Eli, Zacharias, or Caiaphas
12 Record player
14 "__ to your faith virtue" (2 Peter 1:5)
21 Farmer
23 Synthetic resin
24 Dock a boat
25 Jesus "went up __ a mountain to pray" (Luke 9:28 NIV)
27 God's creation

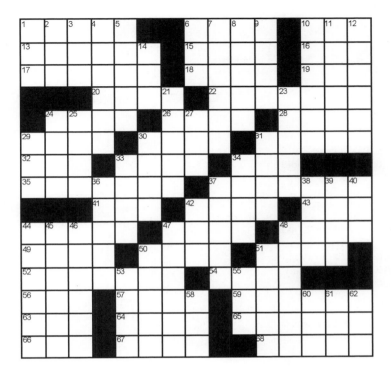

29 God's compassionate ways, for
   short
30 God "__ what is done in secret"
   (Matt. 6:18 NIV)
31 "Law and the Prophets __ on
   these two commandments"
   (Matt. 22:40 NIV)
33 What Jesus forgives
34 Product of Paul's trade
36 Remnant
37 What owner of vineyard did
38 Jesus would soothe it
39 "Did ye never __ in the
   scriptures...?" (Matt. 21:42)
40 Dab
42 Vineyard need, perhaps
44 Choral group
45 List of boo-boos
46 Displayed feeling

47 Clay handler
48 Cloth maker
50 Nile area
51 "O death, where is thy __?"
   (1 Cor. 15:55)
53 Fastener
55 Similar to (2 words)
58 Choose
60 Flightless bird
61 Cusp
62 Blabbermouth would do
   this

37

FOLLOWING HIM

ACROSS

1 Board game
6 Handy household tape
10 Sprite
13 Writer Blaise
15 Crete or Cyprus
16 "Thou art not __ from the kingdom of God" (Mark 12:34)
17 Respiratory ailment
18 Preacher to Gentiles
19 TGIF part (Abbr.)
20 "Now my life __ away" (Job 30:16 NIV)
22 Followers __ in God's Word
24 Writer Bombeck
26 Washington figures
28 Look over
29 "God, do not ignore my __" (Ps. 55:1 NIV)
30 Followers have __ for the future
31 Condemned
32 Belonging to (Suffix)
33 Old story
34 NT time, e.g.
35 Followers __ new members
37 Dot
41 Garden gal
42 "Casting all your __ upon him" (1 Peter 5:7)
43 Veto vote
44 41 Across downfall, traditionally
47 Preacher might stand on one
48 "__ to me, that ye might have life" (John 5:40)
49 Jesus' follower, for short
50 Domestic dog
51 Salad choice
52 26 Across river

54 "He sent them to preach...and to __ the sick" (Luke 9:2)
56 Example for sluggard, per Proverbs
57 Chinese gelatin
59 Leering
63 Devil's statement, e.g.
64 "Woe __ you, ye blind guides" (Matt. 23:16)
65 "Shepherds living out in the fields __" (Luke 2:8 NIV)
66 Digital watch image (Abbr.)
67 "The __ shall be first" (Matt. 19:30)
68 Angel appeared to Joseph in one

DOWN

1 Tax-time helper (Abbr.)
2 KJV's hath
3 Superlative (Suffix)
4 Outline
5 Brazilian dance
6 "Lazarus, that he may __ the tip of his finger in water" (Luke 16:24)
7 Operational
8 Puzzle elements
9 "I __ you the truth" (John 8:45)
10 Result
11 Newly hatched insects
12 "What a __ We Have in Jesus," hymn
14 Big dog, for short
21 Fern seed
23 "God of Abraham, and of __" (Acts 3:13)

24 "Thoughts...accusing or __ excusing one another" (Rom. 2:15)
25 Fisher's need
27 Poet's reveal
29 Sanctuary seat
30 Our heavenly __
31 "Truth shall make you __" (John 8:32)
33 Followers commanded to __ one another
34 Sins
36 Oratorio instrument, perhaps
37 Followers have __ in God
38 Door grip
39 "I Am Jesus' Little __," hymn
40 "Light of the body is the __" (Matt. 6:22)

42 Purrer
44 Revolt
45 Relating to language
46 Pocked
47 Coins, slangily
48 Preacher's neckwear
50 __ Carta
51 Daniel's lions, e.g.
53 Mangle
55 Long, long time
58 "Name of the wicked shall __" (Prov. 10:7)
60 Wrath
61 Athletic group (Abbr.)
62 Workout site

BAPTISM

ACROSS

1 Ship's letters
4 Shrine item, perhaps
9 Shining, like angels
14 Salon feature, often
15 OT or NT time period
16 "__ we were yet sinners, Christ died" (Rom. 5:8)
17 Devil might __ fiery darts
18 He baptized Cornelius
19 Seeped
20 Web action
22 Evils
24 Devil descriptor
25 Church feature
27 27th U.S. president
31 Sicilian erupter
32 Composer Francis __ Key
33 Bible metal
34 Angry
36 End
38 Arrangements
40 Speaker setting
42 "Now are ye __ in the Lord" (Eph. 5:8)
43 Kinder
44 Expert, for short
45 "Word was made flesh, and __ among us" (John 1:14)
47 Scorch
51 Loch __ monster
53 Hawkeye State
54 Mother of Mary, traditionally
55 Baptism ending
57 John the Baptizer's river
59 "No longer a __, but God's child" (Gal. 4:7 NIV)
62 Take exception to

65 Baptized are __ body in Christ
66 Tanker
67 Baptism will __ guilt from soul
68 Gossip
69 Garden tool
70 Tears
71 Joppa to Hebron (dir.)

DOWN

1 Functioning
2 Modern 10 Down
3 South Pacific island dweller
4 Agents, for short
5 Fencing sword
6 Sodom fleer
7 Cube cooler
8 Messiah
9 Unauthorized leave
10 "Baptizing them in the name of...the Holy __" (Matt. 28:19)
11 Screen star Taylor
12 Madrid cheer
13 Say "I do"
21 Apparition
23 "__ us...cast off the works of darkness" (Rom. 13:12)
25 Bible book of many baptisms
26 Poet Edgar Allan
28 Molecule
29 Pentecost's tongues of __
30 Explosive (Abbr.)
32 Maple tree product
35 Trail feature
36 Lager
37 Disciple Judas acted as one
38 Beget
39 Some people have huge ones
40 Handyman Bob

41 Reformation Day mo. (Abbr.)
42 Caregiver's certificate (Abbr.)
43 With 64 Down, what baptized believers put on
45 "Live after the flesh, ye shall __" (Rom. 8:13)
46 Many looked at Jesus with awe and __
48 Baptism __ us with 10 Down
49 Pineapple (Ger.)
50 God will never __ on His promises
52 "Believe and be __" (Luke 8:12)
56 Mary to Jesus (Fr.)
57 "The __ shall live by faith" (Rom. 1:17)
58 Mined metals
59 Steel wool pad brand
60 Mouth part

61 Chicken __ king (2 words)
63 Poetic preposition
64 See 43 Down

39

APOSTLE PAUL

ACROSS

1 Paul's missionary focus
5 Former Russian ruler
9 Opaque gem
13 Twin Cities state (Abbr.)
14 Rant's partner
15 Where Paul left Titus
16 I "am not __ to be called an apostle" (1 Cor. 15:9)
17 Madrid cheers
18 Cut down
19 King who invited Paul to speak (Acts 26)
21 Edible root
23 Peter would cast it into the sea
24 Paul's son in faith, for short
25 Ananias had one concerning Paul
29 Computer choice
30 "Spirit of truth...__ out from the Father" (John 15:26 NIV)
32 Caleb, for one
33 Some Southeast Asians
36 Speak suddenly
37 Retention problem (Abbr.)
38 Paul taught "in the lecture __ of Tyrannus" (Acts 19:9 NIV)
39 I "am less than the __ of all saints" (Eph. 3:8)
40 Funny saying
41 Card game
42 I am "the __ of sinners" (1 Tim. 1:16 NIV)
43 Bloodsucker
44 French possessive
45 Has
46 Seafood choice
47 Peter, in France
49 Corp. department (Abbr.)
50 Recipe measure (Abbr.)
53 Vegetable
55 Lasagna spice
57 "I have made myself a __ to everyone" (1 Cor. 9:19 NIV)
60 Stylish
62 Black
63 With cupbearer in Joseph's prison
64 Garden chore
65 Paul on the road: "Who art thou, __?" (Acts 9:5)
66 Pre-K lessons
67 Eye infection
68 Those Jesus invited to come to Him

DOWN

1 Jordan capital
2 Blockade
3 Static
4 Against
5 __ of Capricorn
6 Arabic peace (var.)
7 "__ Maria"
8 "Power of Christ may __ upon me" (2 Cor. 12:9)
9 Black and white snack
10 Church chair
11 Jesus __ with sinners
12 "As many as are __ by the Spirit of God" are His (Rom. 8:14)
15 Paul, a servant of Jesus __
20 School-year groups (Abbr.)
22 Prevent
26 Problem, in modern parlance
27 Concerning an eye

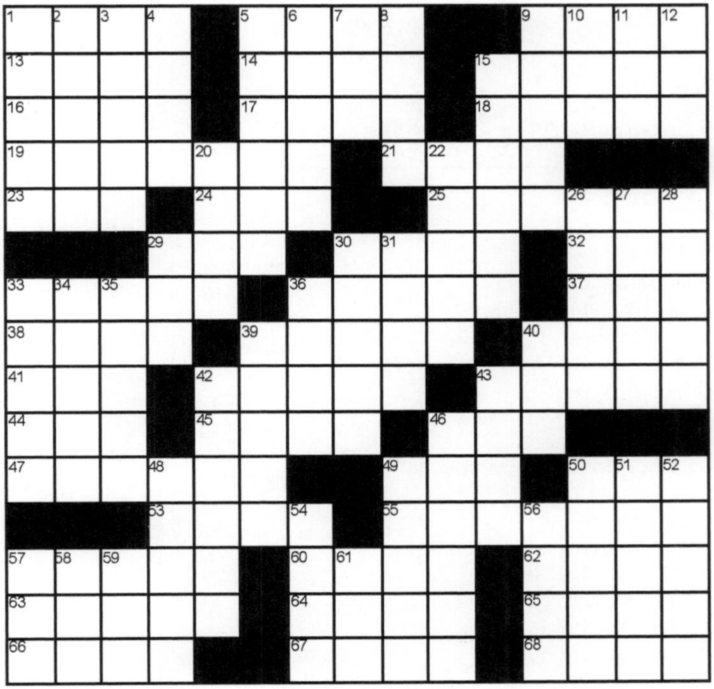

28 Forest dweller of myth
29 Unit of length (Abbr.)
30 "We see through a __, darkly" (1 Cor. 13:12)
31 Kick out
33 Wallop
34 Vietnamese capital
35 "Man shall not live by bread __" (Matt. 4:4)
36 Swiss capital
39 "Thou madest him a little __ than the angels" (Heb. 2:7)
40 It is proven (Abbr.)
42 Philemon, Paul's dear friend and fellow __
43 "Who shall separate us from the __ of Christ?" (Rom. 8:35)
46 "He sits enthroned above the __ of the earth" (Isa. 40:22 NIV)
48 Wanders
49 Crocheted table topper
50 No-no
51 Swine sound
52 Frogs' homes
54 Book written by Luke
56 Money (Ger.)
57 Govt. agency (Abbr.)
58 Popular dog, for short
59 58 Down registry (Abbr.)
61 Smack

40

NEW TESTAMENT LETTERS

ACROSS

1 Natural gelatin
5 Nebraska native
10 Luke, for short
13 Letter writer to Jerusalem church
15 Blot out (2 words)
16 "Eye hath not seen, nor __ heard" (1 Cor. 2:9)
17 Dead to sin, "but __ unto God" (Rom. 6:11)
18 Ship's intake
19 "Pray for them which despitefully __ you" (Luke 6:28)
20 Wonderful, slangily
21 Tribe
23 Permitted
25 "I stand at the __, and knock" (Rev. 3:20)
26 Inhabitant of island 39 Down landed on
28 Letters to seven churches message
31 Mexican coins
32 Leered at
33 Rhizome bloomer
34 Alpine sport
37 Park a boat
38 Sleep disorder
40 "__ is a faithful saying" (1 Tim. 4:9)
41 Approximate amount (Abbr.)
42 Backtalk
43 Fish basket
44 Revelation figure
45 Thresh
46 Dye product
49 Lazarus's wounds, e.g.
50 Put straight
51 Indonesian spot
52 Former fast flyer (Abbr.)
55 "Thy __ and thy staff they comfort me" (Ps. 23:4)
56 Jesus wore one
59 Commandments mount
61 Soap-making need
62 Deliverer of Revelation letters
63 Tots' vehicle, for short
64 Commercials
65 Like Nile's banks
66 You should "__ up the gift of God" (2 Tim. 1:6)

DOWN

1 Slightly open
2 Big to-do
3 Surrounded by
4 Pastor, for short
5 Certain award
6 "We finish our years with a __" (Ps. 90:9 NIV)
7 Easter month, often (Abbr.)
8 Embrace
9 Priscilla and Aquila's mentee (Acts 18:26)
10 Tennis tie
11 Welcome sight in Sinai Desert
12 Where 39 Down left Titus
14 Revelation's topic: __ Coming
22 Abraham's kin
24 "World and __ desires pass away" (1 John 2:17 NIV)
25 KJV hind
26 Mary, e.g. (Fr.)
27 Some letters directed there
28 39 Down wrote a letter to the Christians there

29 Prideful ones
30 "They __ evil against you...they cannot succeed" (Ps. 21:11 NIV)
31 Valentine's Day colors
34 Former NYC stadium
35 Ukrainian capital
36 12 Down is one
38 "We shall __ live with him" (2 Tim. 2:11)
39 Prolific letter writer
40 The cross, figuratively
42 Upscale cafe', maybe (2 words)
43 Anointed One
44 Irish dance
45 Fa follower, musically
46 Waitress on *Cheers*
47 Architect Frank __ Wright
48 Assistants
49 Woefully

51 Left over manna __ worms (Ex. 16:20)
52 Pout
53 Rice wine
54 Level
57 Hydrocarbon suffix
58 "Even to your old __...I am he" (Isa. 46:4)
60 Tax agency

41

BOOK OF JAMES

ACROSS

1 "Grievous words __ up anger" (Prov. 15:1)
5 Judah and Galilee, e.g.
10 "Night is far spent, the __ is at hand" (Rom. 13:12)
13 "Faith without __ is dead" (James 2:20)
15 Eliminate
16 Of a place (Suffix)
17 "We are to God the pleasing __ of Christ" (2 Cor. 2:15 NIV)
18 Mountain climber
19 By way of
20 Commandment number
21 "Surely there is a __ for the silver" (Job 28:1)
23 Nulls
25 "If the __ will, we shall live" (James 4:15)
26 Military uniform feature
28 "We count them happy which __" (James 5:11)
31 __ -garde
32 "Be ye __ of the word" (James 1:22)
33 Cadence
34 Abraham, Isaac and Jacob, e.g.
37 Heredity component
38 __ of the ball
40 Type choice
41 NYC winter hour (Abbr.)
42 "How great a matter a little __ kindleth!" (James 3:5)
43 Shampoo product
44 "Is any __? Let him sing psalms" (James 5:13)
45 Lebanese capital

46 Turin relic and others
49 God's love would __ a troubled soul
50 One of five Jesus suffered, traditionally
51 Wheeze
52 God sought a man who would "stand in the __" (Ezek. 22:30)
55 Shady tree
56 Loafed
59 Oust
61 Gloria in excelsis __
62 Proclaim
63 Wanders
64 "Do not __, my beloved brethren" (James 1:16)
65 Rendezvous
66 Born and __

DOWN

1 Elite crime-fighter team (Abbr.)
2 KJV's rent
3 Jerusalem's gates, e.g.
4 Yarn strength meas. (Abbr.)
5 Rose pest
6 Many an ancient site
7 Exclamation of astonishment
8 Elizabeth conceived in her old __
9 James's word for himself (James 1:1)
10 "Resist the __, and he will flee" (James 4:7)
11 Stage whisper
12 Missing in unleavened bread
14 Relishes

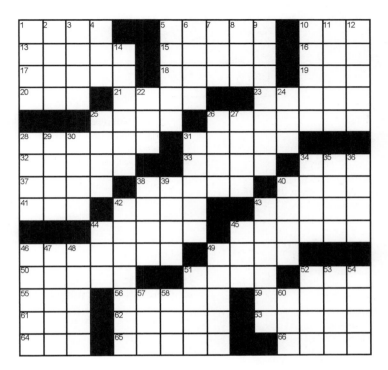

22 "How long will it be __ thou be quiet?" (Jer. 47:6)

24 "__ of the same mouth proceedeth blessing and cursing" (James 3:10)

25 Attract

26 "Speak not __ one of another" (James 4:11)

27 Wan

28 Rim

29 Negatives

30 Bend

31 Pathway

34 Port city feature

35 Freedom org. (Abbr.)

36 "No fountain both yield __ water and fresh" (James 3:12)

38 Sparrow

39 Sins

40 Overly proper

42 Hatfield or McCoy, e.g.

43 Rock thrower

44 Weekday (Abbr.)

45 Make taboo

46 Certain Scandinavian

47 Nine-__, small golf green

48 Unsubstantiated story

49 Plebe

51 Fido and Fluffy

52 Equipment

53 Tip-top

54 Wartime ailment (Abbr.)

57 Rural dragster's sport (Abbr.)

58 Not clerical

60 "Ye have heard of the patience of __" (James 5:11)

BOOK OF HEBREWS

ACROSS

1 Fuel source
5 "Feet __ with...the gospel of peace" (Eph. 6:15)
9 Gossip does this
13 "Salute all them that have the __ over you" (Heb. 13:24)
14 "He will wipe every __ from their eyes" (Rev. 21:4 NIV)
15 52 Down capital
16 Eye
17 Garden tool
18 He was "fully __ in every way" (Heb. 2:17 NIV)
19 God's message "is...__ than any twoedged" 33 Across (Heb. 4:12)
21 Bible, God's __
23 Prodigal son's dwelling, for a time
24 Body art, for short
25 Saudi capital
29 "__, and ye shall receive" (John 16:24)
30 Deer
32 Debtor's note
33 See 19 Across
36 Automaton
37 Total
38 Fur
39 "By faith __,...refused to be called the son of Pharaoh's daughter" (Heb. 11:24)
40 "Holy Ghost __ is a witness to us" (Heb. 10:15)
41 Free of
42 Saunter
43 Drive a car

44 "Cast me not off in the time of old __" (Ps. 71:9)
45 Mimics
46 "The Raven" author
47 "Come boldly unto the __ of grace" (Heb. 4:16)
49 __-ray, disk choice
50 Foot part
53 "God is a consuming __" (Heb. 12:29)
55 Leaning on, as God
57 Spaghetti, e.g.
60 Like Jonah in the fish's belly
62 Courtroom figure (Abbr.)
63 Hurts
64 Short times, for short
65 Horse's sound
66 "Faith is...evidence of things not __" (Heb. 11:1)
67 None but Jesus' sacrifice can __ away sins
68 "I have __ the faith" (2 Tim. 4:7)

DOWN

1 Calvary sight
2 "Holy Ghost shall teach you... what ye __ to say" (Luke 12:12)
3 Relieve
4 Stare
5 Window wipe result, at times
6 "Draw near with a true __" (Heb. 10:22)
7 Absalom hanged on one
8 Used a pencil, maybe
9 Showy
10 Point a weapon
11 Lingerie item
12 Jesus, the __ of God
15 Anointed One

(Crossword puzzle grid with numbered cells)

20 GI ailment
22 Sandwich cookies
26 Church feature
27 Soak
28 Disposition
29 KJV is
30 Medicine amounts
31 "He saves "all them that __ him" (Heb. 5:9)
33 Jack who could eat no fat
34 Listeners "should __ carefully what is said" (1 Cor. 14:29 NIV)
35 "Do not rebuke an __ man harshly" (1 Tim. 5:1 NIV)
36 Jesus __ on the third day
39 Sad-sack
40 Jesus __ with sinners
42 Fads

43 "Hope we have as an anchor of the __" (Heb. 6:19)
46 "Without faith it is impossible to __ him" (Heb. 11:6)
48 "As __ as ye eat this bread, and drink this cup" (1 Cor. 11:26)
49 Classic shampoo brand
50 Hebrews, Romans, or James, e.g.
51 High up (2 words)
52 15 Across nation
54 Where Magi came from
56 Talk on and on
57 Step (Fr.)
58 Get an A
59 Pronoun for Mary or Martha
61 Mediterranean, for one

43

BOOK OF ACTS

ACROSS

1 Experimenter's place
4 Orange gem
9 Financial products (Abbr.)
12 Filler for 28 Across (Sp.)
14 Insect stage
15 Fire need
16 "Hand of the __ was with them" (Acts 11:21)
17 Attempts
18 __ mater
19 Explain Bible verse, e.g.
21 He brought Ethiopian to faith (Acts 8)
23 Droll
24 Beggar "__ for alms at the Beautiful gate" (Acts 3:10)
25 Indian garment
28 Nile, e.g. (Sp.)
31 "In every nation he __ feareth him...is accepted" (Acts 10:35)
34 City of 69 Across
36 Paul and Silas, e.g.
38 Take to court
40 Ukrainian capital
41 Improvise (2 words)
43 Bruins' home
44 Chicken __ king (2 words)
45 "__ unto thee, Chorazin!" (Matt. 11:21)
46 Rhoda would __ she heard Peter's voice (Acts 12:15)
48 Change
51 Sin
53 Site of many early churches
54 Garment for 24 Across
56 Tidal flow
58 What Paul did at 69 Across

61 Bible book: Acts of the __
66 Some listeners gave Paul __ attention
67 Wooden
69 Mars' __, Paul's sermon site
70 Pennsylvania city
71 Prodigal yearned to eat food he fed to __
72 Harvard's rival
73 Time measurement, for short
74 What Paul made for a living
75 Moses parted the __ Sea

DOWN

1 Melodic tra followers (2 words)
2 Competition at Greek games
3 "Did not our heart __ within us?" (Luke 24:32)
4 Paul found one to "Unknown God"
5 Deacon Stephen, e.g.
6 Cheese choice
7 First lady
8 Talks hoarsely
9 Discard
10 Half (Prefix)
11 Strike
13 Disturbance
15 "So were the churches established in the __" (Acts 16:5)
20 Jacob to Esau
22 Bishop's mitre
25 Fence passage
26 I am "straining toward what is __" (Phil. 3:13 NIV)
27 Pulpit figure, for short
29 Couch potato, maybe
30 Affirmative (Fr.)

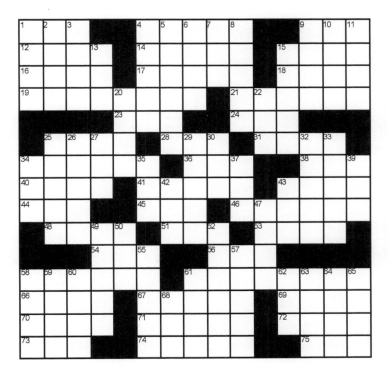

32 Computer code (Abbr.)
33 Oilers' home
34 Wanted poster letters
35 Peter "__ heaven opened"
   (Acts 10:11)
37 Kimono sash
39 Believers "did __ their meat
   with gladness" (Acts 2:46)
42 Buck's mate
43 Ship's letters
47 Captures
49 Some of Paul's listeners
50 Tic __, mint choice
52 "__, and be baptized"
   (Acts 2:38)
55 Holy __, Pentecost figure
57 Jesus' were not broken on
   Calvary
58 White House figure, for short

59 Unusual
60 Acts, for one
61 Like
62 KJV's your
63 Truth is not in one
64 Women's magazine
65 Winter rider
68 "Everyone was filled with __
   at the many...signs"
   (Acts 2:43 NIV)

44

REJOICE!

ACROSS

1 High point
5 Web page
9 Church feature
13 If he takes your shirt, "hand over your __ as well" (Matt. 5:40 NIV)
14 Gesture of disdain
15 Microwave, informally
16 He came to save the __
17 Staring
18 Advanced math class, for short
19 Look "not on what is seen, but on what is __" (2 Cor. 4:18 NIV)
21 He calls all __ to repentance
23 Stumble
25 He brings peace to your __
26 Not (Fr.)
29 He was __ on earth
31 Garden ornament
34 He bids us __ according to His will
35 Cookie aisle product
37 NYC station, for short
39 People __ their cloaks over Jesus' colt
41 Former flyer (Abbr.)
42 Succinct
43 He came to __ our wounds
44 Use a sewing machine
46 People __ palm branches and laid them down
47 Caleb and eleven others
50 Academic dwelling
51 "All you need to say is...__ or No" (Matt. 5:37 NIV)
52 49 Down ingredient, maybe
54 Abraham, Isaac, and Jacob, familiarly
56 Wind farm turbine
59 He teaches us to love __
63 He was called a __ of Jesse
64 Panic
66 Bread spread
67 What Judas may have used
68 Netherland sights
69 Org. (Abbr.)
70 Winter slider
71 Appear
72 "__ have a feast and celebrate" (Luke 15:23 NIV)

DOWN

1 Freedom org. (Abbr.)
2 Masked mammal, for short
3 Roman Catholic worship service
4 Diminutive suffix
5 Modest
6 Eye part
7 North African capital
8 Christmas beverage
9 KJV's wild bull
10 Cat's rumble
11 Winter lodge sights
12 Brain wave test (Abbr.)
14 Elder
20 Funny bone locale
22 Cloistered one
24 "I __ toward the mark for the prize" (Phil. 3:14)
26 He came to light our __
27 He came to soothe our hearts' __
28 Sandal thong
30 Smelled
32 He came to have __ on us

33 Result
36 Razor sharpener
38 Peter and James's fishing needs
40 Prompted
42 "Thou shalt not __ the Lord" (Luke 4:12)
45 Trains for
48 Sin
49 Menu choices
53 Disprove
55 Sandbar
56 Sheep's clothing
57 He came to bring __ to the despairing
58 Eden need, maybe
60 Otherwise
61 He came to bring __ to the weary

62 He came to make us __ of God
63 Some Monopoly properties (Abbr.)
65 Sleep stage (Abbr.)

ACROSS

1 Printer function
5 Press down
9 Play a trumpet, say
13 Angel topper
14 Choir section
15 Ephesian temple goddess (Acts 19)
16 Biblical periods
17 When Jesus dies, the temple veil __
18 Commandment
19 Angel songs
21 Silly one
23 Cost
24 Angel led him from Sodom
25 "Over this way!" (2 words)
29 Flying rodent
30 Ping __ (paddle game)
32 Jesus "made some __ with the saliva" (John 9:6 NIV)
33 Number of angels in Revelation
36 Slurps
37 KJV's art
38 Small bird
39 Surpluses
40 *Anna and the King of* __
41 Charged atom
42 Jerusalem beggars' habitats
43 Gent
44 Gov. food product agency (Abbr.)
45 Angel sat in Jesus' __
46 Stinger
47 Angel with a message
49 __ mode, dessert choice (2 words)
50 __-Magnon, early humans

53 "Good shepherd __ down his life" (John 10:11 NIV)
55 Angels __ God in heaven
57 Angel appearance
60 Arabian peninsula nation
62 Church section
63 Things
64 Angels deliver God's __
65 Device operator
66 Joseph to Baby Jesus
67 Leaf joint
68 Greek letter

DOWN

1 Joseph's was bowed to in his dream
2 Chili con __
3 Angel descriptor
4 Snack
5 Ground squirrel
6 Favorite people
7 Motor oil brand
8 Angels, the heavenly __
9 Angel announced the __ of Jesus
10 He had five loaves and two fish
11 Three Persons, __ God
12 "There was __ in heaven" (Rev. 12:7)
15 Angels' assignments, e.g.
20 Dash
22 Angel features
26 Modern angel's communication method?
27 Outside Jerusalem, say
28 Swelling
29 Jacob's son, for short
30 Perpendicular
31 Reveals

33 Angel's speed
34 Wear away
35 Corrupt
36 Long-faced
39 "__ to God in the highest!"
40 Angels can __ us
42 Unlawfully takes
43 Angels' assurance: "__ not!"
46 Angels in classical art
48 Camel cousin
49 Merit badge
50 Run after
51 Fascinate
52 *Carmen*, for one
54 Seed __ on thorny ground, per parable
56 Rebuff
57 Some looked for a way to get __ of Jesus

58 JFK info (Abbr.)
59 Make-up diploma (Abbr.)
61 Pasture sound

JOURNEYS

ACROSS

1 Gray-haired, maybe
5 Ogle
9 Ukrainian port (var.)
14 Feet after a journey, maybe
15 Red sky in the morning, perhaps
16 Wall hanging
17 Toward 5 Down, a journey of the __
18 Calendar info
19 "Go...and __ all nations" (Matt. 28:19)
20 Computer code letters
22 Mother __
24 Investigator (Abbr.)
25 Some missionaries
27 Press
31 Belle's partner
32 Desire (with "for")
34 Korean flute
35 They journeyed from the East
38 "No seats available" (Abbr.)
40 Less unkind
42 Paradises
44 "__ 'em," dog's command
46 Mission field
47 "Even the __ and the sea obey him!" (Matt. 8:27)
48 Journeyer away from Sodom
50 Story
51 Wide shoe size
52 Bible metal
55 Journeyer's drink, perhaps
57 Scam
59 Non-eater
61 Company (Fr.)
64 25 Across would preach this
66 Skeins
68 African church locale
71 Samoan capital
73 Clue
74 Unfitting
75 Legal claim
76 Robert __, Confederate Army officer (2 words)
77 "Nor height, nor __" can keep us from His love (Rom. 8:39)
78 See 58 Down
79 Mediterranean and Aegean (Fr.)

DOWN

1 Syrian figure
2 Christmas bird
3 Belch
4 Sandwich source
5 17 Across focus
6 Dilettantes
7 Pentecost preacher
8 Spirit-infused power
9 Horse's breakfast
10 Many a journey's motivation
11 New Testament, e.g.
12 Joey's home
13 Brimstone leavings
21 Freezer find
23 "Light of the body is the __" (Matt. 6:22)
26 Melodic syllables
28 Ghana traveler's destination, maybe
29 Shore souvenir
30 Crowd of people
31 "__ him hand and foot" (Matt. 22:13)
33 Vane dir. (Abbr.)
35 Pussy cat

Crossword grid (numbered cells): 1, 2, 3, 4, 5, 6, 7, 8, 9, 10, 11, 12, 13, 14, 15, 16, 17, 18, 19, 20, 21, 22, 23, 24, 25, 26, 27, 28, 29, 30, 31, 32, 33, 34, 35, 36, 37, 38, 39, 40, 41, 42, 43, 44, 45, 46, 47, 48, 49, 50, 51, 52, 53, 54, 55, 56, 57, 58, 59, 60, 61, 62, 63, 64, 65, 66, 67, 68, 69, 70, 71, 72, 73, 74, 75, 76, 77, 78, 79

36 "Bye-bye"
37 DNAs
39 Anointing fluid
41 Itty-bitty bit
43 Speedy travel choice, once
45 More expensive
49 Digit
53 Doubts
54 Incendiary substance
56 "They passed through the Red sea as by __ land" (Heb. 11:29)
58 78 Across destination, once
60 Old photo finish
61 U.S. surgeon George Washington
62 17 Across journey
63 Colorado park
65 Solemn promise
67 "Pssst!"

68 Barnyard baby
69 Hydrocarbon suffix
70 Need after a long journey, maybe
72 "If __ man will come after me" (Matt. 16:24)

47

IN JESUS' TIME

ACROSS

1 Average (Abbr.)
4 His time, a beast of burden
9 Relaxing place
12 49 Down solo
14 He "was dead, and is __ again" (Luke 15:24)
15 Breakfast cereal choice
16 Temple decorators' embellishments
17 Icy rain
18 Pasta option
19 Boney guy
21 61 Across harvest
23 Garment maker would do this
24 __ Father
25 Halt
28 Bethany to Bethlehem (dir.)
31 Observe
34 Squirrels' stash
36 Cart, perhaps, in Jesus' time
38 Game caller, for short
40 In His time, bread-makers' to-do
41 Most tried to __ Roman soldiers
43 Marketplace barter agreement
44 "We __, Abba, Father" (Rom. 8:15)
45 Suffer
46 Lawn-like
48 By __, Jesus' travel option
51 Excitement in marketplace, e.g.
53 Org. (Abbr.)
54 Bottomless __, hell
56 He had five loaves and two fish
58 Plan
61 21 Across concern
66 Many people in His time
67 49 Down approval
69 Jacob's brother
70 Repeated 3 times, WWII movie
71 Anointed
72 Beget
73 Jamaican music genre
74 Extremely heavy
75 Believers are to __ an example

DOWN

1 Droops
2 Laborious journey
3 Coin
4 Social level in His time
5 Permits
6 Appearance
7 Eden gal
8 "You have __ of the commands of God" (Mark 7:8 NIV) (2 words)
9 Seafarer's vessel in His time
10 Fisherman disciple, for short
11 Center of rotation
13 Visual communication (Abbr.)
15 Former Russian rulers
20 Sports channel
22 In His time, herb sometimes tithed
25 In His time, head wrap against sun
26 Japanese capital
27 Mine find
29 Hot liquid burn
30 Bundle
32 Orchard sight in His time
33 40 Across need
34 Network TV channel
35 9 Down milieu
37 In His time, many widows did this

39 Angel's travel option
42 By way of
43 Israelite tribe
47 In His time, donkey owner might do this
49 Musical production
50 Paul's son in faith, for short
52 32 Down fillers
55 Bible "thou shalt not"
57 Current receptor
58 Automotive oil brands
59 Most women did this in His time
60 Israeli circle dance
61 Gorge
62 Affirmative
63 Sale tag info (2 words)
64 Unusual

65 49 Down feature
68 7 Down formed from Adam's

48

LETTERS TO THE CORINTHIANS

ACROSS

1 One shined in the east
5 Wise man's house foundation, per parable
9 "Violent dealing shall come down upon his own __" (Ps. 7:16)
13 Folk singer Guthrie
14 Symphony reed
15 Expedition
16 Moon valley
17 Surrender
18 "Are you not __ of what the law says?" (Gal. 4:21 NIV)
19 In Corinth, preacher with Paul
21 Those who "preach the gospel should __ of the gospel" (1 Cor. 9:14)
23 If in Christ, "he is a __ creature" (2 Cor. 5:17)
24 Summer addition to 37 Across
25 Sluggish
29 E.T.'s ride
30 Pitcher
32 Corinth to Troas (dir.)
33 Conductor Previn
36 Swedish city
37 Four o'clock cuppa
38 Do "not muzzle...the ox that treadeth out the __" (1 Cor. 9:9)
39 Paul preached the __ of Christ
40 "Jesus __," shortest Bible verse
41 Card game
42 Bug spray brands
43 "The __ is the Lord's" (1 Cor. 10:26)
44 Also
45 Teen trouble

46 "Eye hath not seen, nor __ heard" (1 Cor. 2:9)
47 Liveliness
49 One about to graduate (Abbr.)
50 __ Vegas, Nevada
53 Area of early church expansion
55 Most extended
57 "__ be unto you" (1 Cor. 1:3)
60 __ and Span, cleaning brand
62 Galilee or Gennesaret
63 Greased
64 "__ of you has your own gift" (1 Cor. 7:7 NIV)
65 Concluded
66 Not just hearer, but a __
67 Cooler choices
68 Swiss capital

DOWN

1 Wrap brand
2 Cow's belly
3 Permit
4 Jelly or dinner go-with
5 Decorative art style
6 Extremely heavy
7 Fisherman's catch
8 Overturn
9 "Not in word, but in __" (1 Cor. 4:20)
10 Southern constellation
11 Coating for Baby Moses' basket
12 "If the whole body were an __" (1 Cor. 12:17)
15 Party treats
20 "Spirit giveth __" (2 Cor. 3:6)
22 Objects
26 Biblical fisherman
27 Useless

28 "O __, where is thy sting?"
(1 Cor. 15:55)
29 One of many filled with water
at Cana
30 Wash away
31 Weakling
33 Critical
34 "Thou shalt nots"
35 Slump
36 Smile
39 Succulents
40 Armageddon, e.g.
42 Christ was __ from death
43 Work for
46 One who "walked with" 57
Down, and namesakes
48 Competitive runner
49 Dice partner
50 God will never __ you

51 Pray-er, perhaps
52 Strict
54 On 62 Across
56 Lump
57 "Thanks be unto __ for
his...gift" (2 Cor. 9:15)
58 Jordan, e.g. (Sp.)
59 Brew
61 Beatnik's lodgings

49

FAVORITE HYMNS

ACROSS

1 Gas burner
5 "A Poor Wayfaring Man of __"
10 Cooling units (Abbr.)
13 "Amazing __"
15 Insect stage
16 "O God of Love, to Thee We __"
17 God loves a cheerful one
18 Beginning
19 Jesus __ with sinners
20 Exposed (poet.)
21 "__ of Ages"
23 "O Zion, __"
25 "Just a Closer __ with Thee"
26 Ask for seconds, maybe
28 "God's Holy Mountain We __"
31 Spreadsheet
32 Panel
33 Eden tempter's sound
34 "Help!"
37 "I __ to Tell the Story"
38 Fool
40 Cher, formerly
41 Vacation time (Fr.)
42 "Be Still, My __"
43 Constantine's sainted mother
44 26 Across result
45 Machine-human creature
46 Gaps
49 "Old __ Religion"
50 Scrap at Cape Canaveral
51 Whine
52 Layer
55 Offer, as at an auction
56 On a ship (2 words)
59 Ta-ta!
61 Poem
62 Embroidery thread

63 Native
64 King (Lat.)
65 Widely known
66 "__ in the Water"

DOWN

1 Frozen waffle brand
2 Journey
3 Church part
4 Pro
5 Pistol, slangily
6 Prioritize
7 Tax collector (Abbr.)
8 "I Am So Glad Each Christmas __"
9 "Faith of Our __"
10 Demean
11 Terra __, potter's material
12 "In the __ By and By"
14 To-do, perhaps
22 "The __ Rugged Cross"
24 "How Great Thou __"
25 "__ You There?"
26 The Buckeye State
27 "Here Is Love, __ as the Ocean"
28 Qualified
29 Ash residue
30 Grotto
31 "__ of the King"
34 Hymn part, maybe
35 Single individual
36 "My __ Is Love Unknown"
38 Small particle
39 Fees
40 Infant Jesus, e.g. (Fr.)
42 New Mexico capital (2 words)
43 Where to find hymns
44 Big __, California

45 Spy org. (Abbr.)
46 "Come, __ On"
47 "__ with Me"
48 Scripture manuscript
49 1 Down alternative
51 Costa __, California
52 Type choice
53 "__ Kindly Light"
54 Time to sing 8 Down
57 Treat with compassion (Abbr.)
58 Musical scale tone
60 Stock market name

50

POTPOURRI

ACROSS

1 Peter and James's needs
5 Swimming holes
10 "Woman came to him with an alabaster __ of...perfume" (Matt. 26:7 NIV)
13 Entertain
15 Wit
16 Flightless bird
17 Gomer's faithful husband
18 Persian Gulf state
19 Jesus, __ of God
20 "Pray for them which despitefully __ you" (Luke 6:28)
21 34 Down former name
23 Problem, in modern parlance
25 Hell, a lake of __
26 Overlays
28 Comparison image
31 Funeral hymn
32 Infested with plague pests
33 Land measurement
34 Not (Fr.)
37 Ruler segment
38 Those who possess
40 Balaam: "I __ say whatever I please" (Num. 22:38 NIV)
41 Morse code click
42 Indonesian island
43 Fry lightly
44 Bible king
45 Disciple
46 Minus a limb
49 "What __ ye to weep?" (Acts 21:13)
50 Under (poet.)
51 "They that __ soft clothing are in kings' houses" (Matt. 11:8)

52 "With my song will I praise __" (Ps. 28:7)
55 Merry
56 Expect
59 Wash away
61 Gaza to Jerusalem (dir.)
62 North Germanic
63 "He is __!"
64 Soap ingredient
65 "I shall break there the __ of Egypt" (Ezek. 30:18)
66 School groups

DOWN

1 Honolulu's island
2 Tekoan prophet
3 Tactic
4 Megiddo to Jerusalem (dir.)
5 Anger
6 Spoken, as the gospel message
7 Negative
8 Genetics term (Abbr.)
9 Doctor's tool
10 Jesus, Root of __
11 Love (It.)
12 Ancient German letters
14 Love "is not __ angered" (1 Cor. 13:5 NIV)
22 KJV's art
24 "Blessed are your eyes, for they __" (Matt. 13:16)
25 "I will send you out to __ for people" (Mark 1:17 NIV)
26 Immoral pursuit
27 Sins
28 Stumbled on ice
29 Inner Hebrides island

30 "Prayer of a righteous man avai-
   leth __" (James 5:16)
31 OT king
34 See 21 Across
35 Against
36 "Let us keep in __ with the
   Spirit" (Gal. 5:25 NIV)
38 Tortoise's competitor
39 Brought to Jesus' tomb
40 First murderer
42 Mary and Martha's home
43 Selfless giver
44 Poor man's abode
45 It's in a pod
46 Holy messenger
47 Ill-tempered person
48 Cash recipient
49 Doles out

51 "Who then is the faithful
   and __ servant?"
   (Matt. 24:45 NIV)
52 "Suddenly there was...the
   heavenly __ praising God"
   (Luke 2:13)
53 Notion
54 Don't be "a busybody in
   other __ matters"
   (1 Peter 4:15)
57 Date
58 __ of the Covenant
60 Tear apart

OLD TESTAMENT BOOKS

ACROSS

1 Place of torment
6 Tear, as Psalm 7:2 NIV
9 __ vu
13 Arena shapes
14 Stray, as Psalm 95:10
15 Trial watcher
16 Hearing, smell, e.g.
17 Dove's call
18 With 25 Across, ark flyers, perhaps
19 New York canal
20 Tent fabric
22 Backbiting, as Proverbs 25:23 NIV
23 Dined
24 Breach
25 See 18 Across
27 David __ the stone at Goliath
29 Flowerlike formation
33 Ruth __ down beside Boaz
34 Pilates targets
35 Air (Prefix)
36 Knights' competition
39 " __ banner over me was love" (Song 2:4)
40 "Envy__ the simple" (Job 5:2 NIV)
41 Throw out
42 Beaver's building
43 Hind's partner
44 Winds
46 Chilean mountains
49 Decisive defeat
50 18 Across concern
51 Fate of aging eyes
53 Klutz
56 Worthless
58 Antic
59 Fairy tale writing brothers
61 "Thou shalt __ , but not be satisfied…" (Micah 6:14)
62 Caravan stopping place
63 "I know that my redeemer __"
64 Pronoun for Esther
65 It's not good for man to be __
66 Adam's garden
67 Day before Wed.
68 2 OT books by this name

DOWN

1 Prophet who loved Gomer
2 Prevents
3 OT prophet
4 "I am the Lord your God, and none __" (Joel 2:27)
5 Jerusalem to Carmel (dir.)
6 Review
7 Elisha made it float
8 Book of wise sayings
9 Made a well
10 14 Across (pl.)
11 Prophet whose name means "Jehovah is God"
12 Pretentious
15 Foretold in OT
20 Artful
21 Prophet from Tekoa
24 "You strain out a __ but swallow a camel"
26 Certified, as Esther 3:12
28 Northern Ireland
30 Earl Grey or Oolong
31 " __ me, and know my thoughts" (Ps. 139:23)
32 Dawn goddess at Athens
34 Point

36 Satan tested him
37 Adam and Eve pronoun
38 Utilize
39 Brashest
40 __ of Solomon
42 5th OT book
43 "Why do the heathen __ ...?"
   (Ps. 2:1)
45 Soars
47 Prolific inventor Thomas
48 Building material
50 __ Lauder cosmetics
52 Exodus figure
53 Stare at
54 Describes wilderness
55 Number of books in Pentateuch
57 Honolulu island

58 Painter of melting clocks
60 Obadiah, Boaz, e.g.
62 Gideon's tree

GENESIS

ACROSS

1 Honey homes
6 Military school (Abbr.)
10 "We cry '__, Father'"(Rom. 8:15)
14 Ephesus marketplace
15 "Ali __ and the Forty Thieves"
16 Derogatory remark, as in Ps. 15:3 NIV
17 "Thy brother's __ crieth unto me" (Gen. 4:10)
18 Abraham, financially
19 Lotion brand
20 "The Lord God __ him out of... Eden" (Gen. 3:23 NKJV)
21 Created on Day 6
22 Texas or Ukraine city
24 A mark kept Cain from this
26 In the middle
27 Postpones
30 "I led them with... __of love" (Hos. 11:4 NIV)
31 Woman will not "__ authority" over man (1 Tim. 2:12)
32 Ephod stone
33 Adam, Enos, e.g.
36 Parsonage
37 Downwind, as Acts 27:4 NIV
38 Egg-shaped
40 Unopened flower
41 Magnificent
43 Tabernacle curtain components
44 Juicy Fruit and Dentyne
45 Arctic outerwear
46 It drove Abram to Egypt
49 West African nation
50 "I will make of thee a great __" (Gen. 12:2)
51 Amount, as Num. 1:2

52 "__ is mount Sinai in Arabia" (Gal. 4:25)
56 Aaron's expression of woe (Num. 12:11)
57 Egyptian wader
59 Travelocity spokesman
60 Patmos or Malta (poet.)
61 Faithful ark builder
62 Bitter
63 Stare
64 Musky
65 Moses did mighty ones (Acts. 7:22)

DOWN

1 Taxis
2 Gawk
3 Night-light
4 Joseph's betrayed him
5 Nehemiah's countenance
6 Father of nations
7 Abel's slayer
8 TV network
9 Former name for Benin
10 "Jesus __, 'Who do you say that I am?'"
11 God promises to __ Abram (Gen. 12:2)
12 "__ into song, you mountains" (Isa. 49:13 NIV)
13 Opera solo
21 Sarah to Abraham (Abbr.)
23 Unfaithful, as Ps. 78:57 NIV
25 Chord type
26 Voiced
27 Jesus "maketh...the __ to speak" (Mark 7:37)
28 Jacob's twin

29 Finance
30 Shadrach and Daniel age range
32 "We should be holy and without __" (Eph. 4:4)
33 Third Gospel
34 Italy volcano
35 G-man Eliot
39 A work of the flesh (Gal. 5:20)
42 Ceremonial water (Lev. 14:5)
45 Brand of non-stick spray
46 "Thou shalt not bear __
   witness" (Ex. 20:16)
47 Our years are "__ that is told"
   (2 words) (Ps. 90:9)
48 "Do not eat the bread of a __"
   (Prov. 23:6 NKJV)
49 Soft
50 Jael's weapon (Judg. 4:22)
51 *The King and I* locale

53 Ox or bull might do this
54 "God has ascended __
   shouts of joy" (Ps. 47:5 NIV)
55 Cincinnati baseball team
58 Snake
59 Son of Jacob and Leah

53

CREATION

ACROSS

1 Hurt
6 David's was a stone
10 "We cry, __, Father" (Rom. 8:15)
14 Kashmiri language
15 "__ not on your own understanding"
16 "__ me in a plain path" (Ps. 27:11)
17 Created in the beginning
18 Jepthah surrounded by one (Judg. 11:3 NIV)
19 God called the dry __ Earth
20 Geographic region
21 "Of every tree…thou mayest freely __" (Gen. 2:16)
22 *Aida* and *Don Giovanni*
24 Central church part
26 Frau's dress
27 Bargain
30 "This is now __ of my bones" (Gen. 2:23)
31 The Lord sent Israel into __
32 Line dance
33 Anointed toe (Lev. 8:23 NIV)
36 Tigris is one
37 The Lord our God is __ (Sp.)
38 Statement of faith
40 Emmaus to Bethany (dir.)
41 One like him of Proverbs 23:21
43 Gabriel's "Greetings!" today
44 Same cite as previous (Lat.)
45 God's "activity" on the seventh day
46 Craftsman's activity
49 Asked, KJV-style
50 Grubby
51 Morning and evening, first __
52 Nerve fiber
56 What spider does to fly
57 Spring flower
59 "I will __ them out from before thee" (Ex. 23:30)
60 Eve's garden
61 Pharaoh's river
62 Colder
63 Bird's home
64 Ark of covenant adornment
65 Trees created this day

DOWN

1 Job asked, "Am I a __?" (Job 7:12)
2 Burn, as brimstone
3 Payment, KJV-style
4 Trap, as Matt. 22:15
5 With 59 Down, Morse Code signal
6 Found in second day creation
7 Herbs were this in Genesis 1
8 Created on Day 6
9 Continuing
10 *Toy Story* Tim
11 Adam's facial hair
12 Unoriginal
13 "To his sin he __ rebellion" (Job 34:37 NIV)
21 Adam's wife
23 Jesus "__ the word unto them" (Mark 2:2)
25 Notifying
26 Giver
27 Pronoun for 21 Down
28 17 Across turns on this
29 "God set them in the firmament… to __ light" (Gen. 1:17)

30 Removed the bones
32 Roman god of love
33 "Can you loosen Orion's __?" (Job 38:31 NIV)
34 "An __ soul shall suffer hunger" (Prov. 19:15)
35 "God saw that it was __" (Gen. 1:10)
39 Study
42 "Ye have purified your souls in __ the truth" (1 Peter 1:22)
45 Seen on first day, __ of light
46 Overly proper one
47 Decoys
48 Concerning
49 The law is not __ on faith

50 Valley (poet.)
51 Tithing spice
53 Number of cities tribes got (Rom.)
54 "Let them have dominion __ ... all the earth" (Gen. 1:26 KJV)
55 Smart person (slang)
58 Nile or Jordan (Sp.)
59 See 5 Down

ANIMALS

ACROSS

1 Dismay (variant)
6 Dog food brand
10 "Will the unicorn be willing to... abide by thy __?" (Job 39:9)
14 Water bird
15 In __ of (instead)
16 Parable guests found here (sing.)
17 Slogan
18 Annoying insect
19 Meshach destination
20 Eden angel held one (Fr.)
21 "Appointed unto men once to __" (Heb. 9:27)
22 Distract
24 "__ me in thy truth" (Ps. 25:5)
26 Mouse, e.g.
27 Nebuchadnezzar's temporary fate
30 Moses removed one at Sinai
31 Speaks with a hoarse voice
32 *Phantom of the __*
33 LP meas.
36 Tiny island
37 Flying 26 Across
38 Queen of Sheba headwear, perhaps
40 Pronoun for Eve
41 Deflect
43 Block of metal
44 Elephant's "tooth"
45 Insect of Egypt
46 "Come ye...and rest __" (Mark 16:31) (2 words)
49 Computer drop-down
50 "He shall __ thy paths" (Prov. 3:6)
51 See 26 Across

52 Ursa of Isaiah 11:7
56 Dead flies cause (Eccl. 10:1)
57 Benjamin and Abner became one (2 Sam. 2:25)
59 Brazilian dance
60 Oppose
61 Memorization technique
62 Pisa tower position
63 First animal site
64 Rebekah filled at the well
65 Roman goddess

DOWN

1 Zenith
2 Support
3 Elisha's was bald
4 Clean animal of Deuteronomy 14:6
5 King of beasts (Lat.)
6 Chilly
7 Rahab's was scarlet
8 Green soup
9 "Put your __ work in order" (Prov. 24:27 NIV)
10 Garlic part
11 Elijah's feeder, once
12 Inactive
13 Prepped a bow
21 Animals created on fifth __
23 Imagination
25 Joyful
26 Scarlett's husband
27 Part of the eye
28 Destroy, as Ps. 2:9
29 John's home, __ of Patmos
30 James 3 fire starter (NIV)
32 Eglon descriptor (Judg. 3:17)
33 Meat-based sauce

(Crossword grid)

34 Cons opposite
35 Disciple's nickname
39 Hen birthing process
42 Carcass eater
45 "__ me not be ashamed" (Ps. 25:2)
46 Helped
47 "Moses __ all the words of the Lord" (Ex. 24:4)
48 Long-legged bird
49 Mary to Jesus (Lat.)
50 Ark flyer
51 Passover, e.g.
53 Eastern ruler
54 Jesus is __ to save us

55 Philistine destroyers (1 Sam. 6:4 NIV)
58 "This is __ bone of my bones" (Gen. 2:23)
59 Pocket

55

THE GARDEN OF EDEN

ACROSS

1 Moses wrote just one
6 Plants were Adam and Eve's
10 Eye infection
14 Forbidden (var.)
15 Paul describes his speech as (2 Cor. 11:6)
16 Sailor "Hi" to Jonah, maybe
17 Eve created while Adam did this
18 "The law is good if one __ it lawfully" (1 Tim. 1:8 NKJV)
19 __ of fire
20 PC key
21 Take away
23 Where Israelites dwelt
25 Sausage
26 First woman
27 Be next to
30 Chihuahua (2 words)
34 Daniel and Mary age range
35 A __ wind blew away locusts (Ex. 10:19)
36 "Will a man __ God?" (Mal. 3:8)
38 Group of eight
39 Lyricist David
40 Musical composition
42 Sleeping rug
43 What Esau hunted
44 Accepted practice
45 Luke's study sites, perhaps
48 Tools for Jesus, perhaps
49 Iron is one
50 Sheep attacker
51 Grew in Eden post-Fall
54 Mite or penny
55 Gas mileage grp.
58 German mister
59 France & Germany river
61 What locusts do to crops (2 words)
63 Allotted portion
64 Tree of knowledge of good and __
65 Encourages, __ on
66 Adam used to till garden
67 "He shall __ his angel before thee" (Gen. 24:7)
68 Steps for crossing a fence

DOWN

1 Battle-related illness (Abbr.)
2 Abraham/Hittites transaction
3 Adam's son
4 Chop
5 Driver
6 Plentiful in Eden
7 Expel, like Adam and Eve
8 "__ on a Grecian Urn"
9 Lineage
10 Seasoned, as Mark 9:49
11 Pad __
12 Jesus, "My __ is easy" (Matt. 11:30)
13 Adam and Eve's were opened
22 Made in God's image
24 __ League school
25 "This is now __ of my bones" (Gen. 2:23)
27 Molecule
28 Decorative sticker
29 Jonah's departure point
30 Oxen pairs
31 Patmos or Cyprus
32 Psalmist's instrument, as Genesis 4:21
33 See 48 Across (sing.)
35 Smack

37 Buzzers Samson found
40 "In Your presence is __ of joy" (Ps. 16:11 NKJV)
41 Flying military branch (Abbr.)
43 Samson riddle responses
46 David's horse's home
47 Suffix indicating direction
48 Taro dish
50 "For God so loved the __" (John 3:16)
51 "It is not good __ man should be alone" (Gen. 2:18)
52 Goliath to Philistines
53 Favorite dipping cookie
54 See 3 Down
55 Decorative needle case
56 Knitting stitch
57 Church niche

60 Hail (Lat.)
62 Bishop should be "__ to teach" (1 Tim. 3:2)

ACROSS

1 Opposed (Prefix)
5 Policeman
8 Noah's likely hair color
12 Floating ice
13 Cowboy show
15 Soliders put a purple one on Jesus
16 It fell for forty days and nights
17 Forty-first day, Flood __
18 Thought
19 Occupied lodgings
21 Highest opposite
23 Element
25 Bible ender (Abbr.)
26 *Downton* __
29 Crimson
31 Correspond
35 Roman ruler
37 Ark covering
39 Noah's bird
40 Western country (Abbr.)
41 Unicorn of the sea
44 Free of
45 Ascend
47 Also
48 Cursed
50 Communion table
52 Before, KJV-style
54 Authoritarian
55 Flee
57 Seasoning brand
59 Grants an extension
62 Ark landing spot
65 "For thee __ I seen righteous before me" (Gen. 7:1)
66 "Be holy and without __ before him" (Eph. 1:4)
68 U.S. mil. org.
70 Car rental agency
71 Some ark passengers
72 Rudimentary 50 Across
73 Soften
74 NJ neighbor
75 Story

DOWN

1 Edited (Abbr.)
2 "Better is a neighbour that is __ than a brother far off" (Prov. 27:10)
3 Shadrach, Meshach, Abednego
4 "Whoever __ correction leads others astray" (Prov. 10:17 NIV)
5 Ark flyer, perhaps
6 Unusual
7 Apple's skin
8 The Lord "was __ ...at His heart" (Gen. 6:6)
9 Walking sticks
10 A wager (2 words)
11 Yes, Shakespeare-style
13 "A bruised __ shall he not break" (Isa. 42:3)
14 Smell
20 Ancient culture
22 Spider's home
24 Computer sharing system
26 Sporty car brand
27 Italian herb
28 Animal
30 Telegraphic signal
32 Eating utensils
33 Hollies partners
34 Mr. Roosevelt, to friends
36 Unclean gnawer (Lev. 11:29 NIV)

38 Unfinished
42 Hind's mate
43 Zodiac sign
46 Devout
49 Earth's pre-Flood condition
51 Tithing herb
53 Tooth protector
56 Babylon to Nineveh (dir.)
58 Mined metals
59 Rant
60 See 49 Down
61 Skidded
63 Paul preached here
64 Describes Goliath
65 Noah's son
67 "__, King of the Jews" (Lat.)
69 Charge

57

ABRAHAM

ACROSS

1 Sarai claimed she was Abe's (Abbr.)
4 "Wounds __ away evil" (Prov. 20:30 NIV)
9 "There are no __ in their death" (Ps. 73:4)
14 Tyre to Sidon (dir.)
15 Marry secretly
16 Witless
17 Jesus' shipboard nap spot
18 "Flame of fire out of the __ of a bush" (Ex. 3:2)
19 Land Joseph ruled
20 Cat toy stuffing
22 Unclean animal
24 Every __ shall bow
25 Reuben said, "__ no blood" (Gen. 37:22)
27 "God will provide himself a __" (Gen. 22:8)
31 "Does he not...count my every__?" (Job 31:4 NIV)
32 Paul's ship needs
33 Ghost's greeting
34 Leg parts bitten by serpents (Gen. 49:17)
36 Church display place
38 Already fixed in place
40 Abram's home
42 Harriet Beecher __
43 Egyptian days of mourning
44 Angels did with Abraham
45 Hawthorne house part
47 Moses' were bare on Sinai
51 "There was __ of glass like unto crystal" (Rev. 4:6) (2 words)
53 Paul forbidden to preach here
54 David's instrument
55 Gold one held incense
57 Lobbies
59 American writer and politician Sinclair
62 Texas stew
65 Abel's sacrifice
66 Abraham's descendants like these
67 Relating to the ear
68 North American Indian
69 Daniel heard one speaking (Dan. 8:13)
70 Storks' are in fir trees (Ps. 104:17)
71 Hagar's son, e.g.

DOWN

1 Munches
2 "The __ of the poor is seized for a debt" (Job 24:9 NIV)
3 Bench
4 Half (Prefix)
5 "Do not...__ off the edges of your beard" (Lev. 19:27 NIV)
6 Aaron's blossomed
7 Down's opposites
8 Where Jacob dwelt
9 Jonah's departure point
10 Holy messenger
11 Visitor to Sarah, "__; but thou didst laugh" (Gen. 18:15)
12 U.S. economic meas.
13 The Lord __ a mark upon Cain
21 Lot to Abraham
23 Spots
25 Lot's wife's fate
26 Pronoun for Abraham
28 "We cry, __, Father" (Rom. 8:15)
29 Time Abraham stood before the

Lord (poet.)
30 Hagar said, "I cannot watch the __ die" (Gen. 21:16 NIV)
32 "Taste and __ that the Lord is good" (Ps 34:8)
35 Hebron to Masada (dir.)
36 "Go to the __, thou sluggard" (Prov. 6:6)
37 Pond flyer
38 Parent groups (Abbr.)
39 Learn by repetition
40 Coca- __
41 "These __ the...years of Abraham's life" (Gen. 25:7)
42 Abraham's descendants as the sand of this
43 Crime-solving agency (Abbr.)
45 Car feeder
46 Waste bin

48 Dazzler
49 List of mistakes
50 "Some time later God __ Abraham" (Gen. 22:1 NIV)
52 "Then __ yourself with glory and splendor" (Job 40:10 NIV)
56 Research facility, e.g. (Abbr.)
57 "Balaam...fell __ on his face" (Num. 22:31)
58 Used for anointing
59 Ship initials
60 School group (Abbr.)
61 __ Chi
63 Joseph's coat had many a __
64 Tax agency (Abbr.)

ISAAC

ACROSS

1 Sun and moon (poet.)
5 Toothbrush brand
10 Utah or Maine site (Abbr.)
13 Seasoned rice
15 Happen again
16 Second day of week
17 Swelling
18 San __, California
19 Tap
20 __ Testament
21 Daniel's age group
23 Curt
25 Gomorrah fire result
26 Isaac's half-brother
28 Sarah to Isaac
31 Parisian goodbye
32 Jacob felt for Rachel (Fr.)
33 Eden tree, perhaps
34 Shake head
37 Offering animal
38 Isaac's father
40 "Fear not __ down into Egypt" (Gen. 46:3) (2 words)
41 Mamre to Moriah (dir.)
42 Coffee alternative
43 South Korea capital
44 Wading bird
45 How camels travel
46 Asian citrus fruits
49 Hagar resting spot
50 Holy, set __
51 Abraham's became many nations
52 Eliezer was __ to Rebekah
55 Esau's coloring
56 Wrathful
59 Take off
61 Baseball stat

62 Adam & Eve early state
63 Saul saw David as one
64 Offering in Isaac's place
65 Mouse mastications
66 Hawaiian island

DOWN

1 "I have set before thee an __ door" (Rev. 3:8)
2 Isaac's horse purpose
3 Walls fell when trumpets __
4 Prophet's nickname
5 "Let all things be done...in __" (1 Cor. 14:40)
6 Isaac's horse control
7 Genius
8 Tote
9 Abel to Cain
10 Planet's shadow
11 To marinade
12 Heavenly messenger
14 Abraham to Isaac
22 To listen, give __
24 Ark's flightless bird
25 Israel's enemy (Ezek. 30:5)
26 Athenians loved a new one (Acts 17:20 NIV)
27 Thailand, once
28 Isaac, Adam, e.g.
29 Saudi Arabia neighbor
30 Volume, as Ps. 40:7
31 Adam"s response to 62 Across (Gen. 3:7)
34 Used for Isaac sacrifice
35 Flu
36 Given to Rebekah
38 Air (Prefix)
39 Esau and Jacob (Abbr.)

Grid (numbered cells):
1 2 3 4 · 5 6 7 8 9 · 10 11 12
13 · · · 14 · 15 · · · · 16 · ·
17 · · · · 18 · · · · 19 · ·
20 · · · 21 22 · · · · 23 24 · ·
· · 25 · · · · 26 27 · · · ·
28 29 30 · · 31 · · · · · ·
32 · · · · 33 · · · 34 35 36
37 · · · 38 39 · · · 40 · ·
41 · · · 42 · · · 43 · ·
· · 44 · · · 45 · · · ·
46 47 48 · · · 49 · · · ·
50 · · · 51 · · · 52 53 54
55 · · 56 57 58 · · 59 60 · · ·
61 · · 62 · · · · 63 · · ·
64 · · 65 · · · · 66 · · ·

40 Joseph's coat color, perhaps
42 Attacking
43 Braze
44 Pronoun for Sarah
45 Confederate general
46 Small knife
47 Musical production
48 Woman
49 Burnt grass (Matt. 13:30 NIV)
51 Meal for Isaac
52 Found atop Sinai, perhaps
53 Jacob's twin
54 Sandwich spot (Abbr.)
57 Esau __ to meet Jacob
58 Saul, __ Paul
60 Edge

59

JACOB

ACROSS

1 Christianity, at first
5 Capital of Ghana
10 One of Jacob's sons
13 Beside, as Numbers 22:1 NIV
15 Harvested, as James 5:4 NIV
16 Battle of __ Jima
17 He preceded Paul at Athens
18 Cable TV network
19 2,000 pounds
20 Jacob stopped at Bethel when the sun __
21 Jonah's manmade conveyance
23 Brand of tile game
25 "He shall open, and none shall __" (Isa. 22:22)
26 Ivory seats of Ezekiel 27:6
28 Great fish's "teeth," perhaps
31 Tubes
32 It's full of swimmers
33 West Point (Abbr.)
34 Drain, as in Leviticus 26:16 NIV
37 Cleaned up
38 Japanese verse
40 It became lice in Exodus 8:16
41 Jacob's fire residue
42 Samuel title
43 Customs
44 Impersonation
45 Jacob fled here
46 Princess Leia's beau (2 words)
49 "Jacob said, __ me this day thy birthright" (Gen. 25:31)
50 Rejoice
51 Indebted to
52 "The lot is cast into the __" (Prov. 16:33)
55 Eve made of this bone
56 Boys did to Elisha
59 Remove, as Joshua 5:15
61 A bit
62 Swift flier
63 Fancy boat
64 Describes Eden serpent
65 Sag
66 Jacob's kids played with, maybe

DOWN

1 Trees' "blood"
2 Pronoun for Rachel (Fr.)
3 Joseph's was multicolored
4 Dynamite (Abbr.)
5 Jericho's wall formed one
6 Mil. rank
7 Media labor union (Abbr.)
8 Last Bible book (Abbr.)
9 How Rachel was dressed
10 Hole to fall into
11 Jacob did after dreaming
12 Sins (slang)
14 Land given to Jacob's sons
22 Attila the __
24 Coolers (Abbr.)
25 Stool
26 Chicken's "hello," perhaps
27 Jacob's twin
28 __ fide
29 Experts
30 Jacob's first wife
31 Esau's condition
34 "The testimony of the Lord is __" (Ps. 19:7)
35 Part of John's vision (Rev. 4:6) (2 words)
36 Anxiety issue (Abbr.)
38 Jacob grabbed Esau's

39 Air (Prefix)
40 Girl's toy
42 Jacob's cattle type
43 Somewhat
44 Deaf communication (Abbr.)
45 First letter of Genesis
46 Groups of animals
47 Lengthwise
48 Lumpy
49 Use a broom
51 Scandinavian capital
52 Nebuchadnezzar for a time (Sp.)
53 Sackcloth-wearer may look this way
54 Domesticated animals

57 "He who has an __ let him hear" (Rev. 2:11)
58 Past time: long __
60 Jacob fed cattle (sing.)

JOSEPH

ACROSS

1 Commercial (Abbr.)
5 Primary
10 "So be strong, __ like a man" (1 Kings 2:2 NIV)
13 Crop waterers
15 Sporty car brand
16 Tithing herb
17 Many
18 Brew
19 Time period
20 Egypt to Ethiopia (dir.)
21 Timothy's grandmother
23 Joseph's had many colors
25 "You meant __ ...but God meant...good" (Gen. 50:20 NKJV)
26 Potiphar's boss
28 Embroidery type
31 Jacob was told Joseph had been __
32 Potiphar role
33 Grain in Joseph's dream
34 Honey maker
37 Winglike
38 Extent
40 Author Angelou
41 Joseph bro.
42 Cat's greeting
43 Jailed with Joseph
44 Punitive
45 Compulsion
46 Impressionist Mary
49 Potiphar's betrayed Joseph
50 Vigorously (arch.)
51 See 43 Across
52 Jazz type, Be __
55 Joseph's low point
56 Gem State

59 Where Joseph ruled
61 Egypt to Canaan (dir.)
62 Pre-creation earth (Lat.)
63 Wages
64 Shepherd carries one
65 By __ you have been saved
66 Prep a bow

DOWN

1 Joseph "threw his __ around his father and wept" (Gen. 46:29 NIV)
2 Smear mortar
3 Corrupt, as Job 40:4
4 Holy Spirit power is like (Abbr.)
5 Herb
6 Luke's epistle
7 Woman of Luke 8:3, to friends
8 Wrath
9 Potiphar, __ of the guard
10 Some die here (1 Cor. 4:9 NIV)
11 Oddity
12 "__ me thy way, O Lord" (Ps. 27:11)
14 Payment for Joseph
22 Olive or anointing
24 Water holder at Cana (syn.)
25 24 Down synonym
26 Plunk down
27 Unclean hopper
28 Unclean seafood
29 Joseph's destiny, to __ Egypt
30 Zeal
31 Judah's look toward Joseph, perhaps
34 43 Across job
35 How Joseph saw Jacob
36 33 Across holders

38 "God __ me before you to pre-serve you" (Gen. 45:7)
39 See 23 Across (var.)
40 Pharaoh's horse, perhaps
42 Dreams have them (Gen. 40:5 NIV)
43 Cushion
44 Twenty-third letter in Athens
45 "It is appointed unto men once to __" (Heb. 9:27)
46 Jump
47 __ acid
48 Well-fed
49 "I will praise thee with my __ heart" (Ps. 138:1)
51 Stylish
52 Computer memory unit

53 "He shall __, and none shall shut" (Is. 22:22)
54 Anxiety condition (Abbr.)
57 Choir leader (Abbr.)
58 Expression of surprise
60 Talk

MOSES

ACROSS

1 Florida city
6 National Rifle __ (Abbr.)
10 Patmos is one
14 Abraham's son
15 "Delight thyself __ in the Lord" (Ps. 37:4)
16 All right
17 "From the __ born of Pharaoh" (Ex. 12:29)
18 Ephod had four __ of gems
19 Missile, for short
20 Offering bits
21 __ Jones Industrial average
22 Followed
24 "I have set before thee an __ door" (Rev. 3:8)
26 Hebrew work products
27 Turn
30 Seventh plague
31 Plowed, as Deuteronomy 21:4
32 Rachel descriptor (Fr.)
33 Christmas month (Abbr.)
36 Worship
37 Sturdy tree
38 "Superman" actor Christopher
40 __ Commandments
41 "Hatred __ up strife" (Prov. 10:12 NKJV)
43 Eyed
44 Slope
45 Car's "heart"
46 Eve, Sarah, e.g. (slang)
49 It happened: it came to __
50 Girlie
51 VW or Ford, e.g.
52 "We must __ a feast unto the Lord" (Ex. 10:9)
56 Good comes to those who "__ freely" (Ps. 112:5 NIV)
57 Evils
59 Ezekiel's visions, to some
60 Secure, at __
61 Orderly
62 Harvest
63 Lion's home (2 words)
64 Cowboy Autry
65 "Ye shall see the __ of the Lord" (Ex. 16:7)

DOWN

1 Squabble
2 Mount Sinai continent
3 Marketplace
4 Jewish holiday
5 "All who are prudent __ with knowledge" (Prov. 13:16 NIV)
6 Moses' brother
7 "I am __ of speech" (Ex. 4:10)
8 Beersheba to Mount Sinai (dir.)
9 Nose part
10 Greek architecture
11 Prowl
12 Fishing spots
13 Looked at
21 Mid-Atlantic state (Abbr.)
23 Pilot-controlled airfoils
25 Idol holder
26 Resists
27 Temple part: Mercy __
28 Way to cross streams
29 Chariot metal
30 Pharaoh hardened his
32 Sixth plague

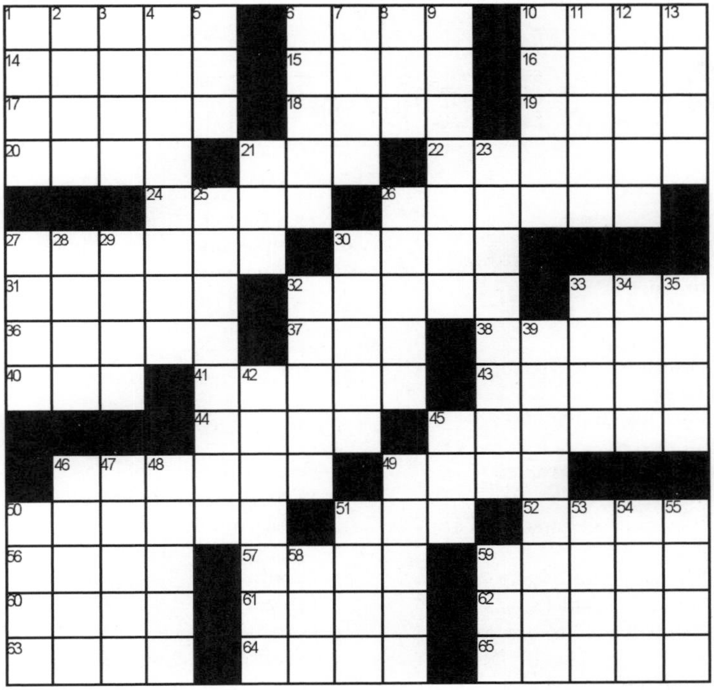

1
2
3
4
5
6
7
8
9
10
11
12
13
14
15
16
17
18
19
20
21
22
23
24
25
26
27
28
29
30
31
32
33
34
35
36
37
38
39
40
41
42
43
44
45
46
47
48
49
50
51
52
53
54
55
56
57
58
59
60
61
62
63
64
65

33 Sandwich shop
34 "Israel is my son, __ my first-born" (Ex. 4:22)
35 Surrender
39 Part of 59 Down
42 Cleaning up
45 Pierced body part
46 4 Down unleavened food
47 Wash cycle
48 __ days
49 Glue
50 Tiny insect
51 Tribe
53 Brand of sandwich cookie
54 Prevaricator
55 __ yourself. Take up His cross.
58 Downwind
59 Hen's concern

EXODUS-OUT OF EGYPT

ACROSS

1 David's was stones (Abbr.)
5 Imitated
9 Bible flyer
14 Satan is one
15 Health partner (Jer. 33:6)
16 Tycoon
17 Preacher Graham Lotz
18 Study
19 Passover's unleavened
20 My (Fr.)
21 They pulled Pharaoh's chariot
23 Has
24 Peter at Pentecost, e.g.
26 She gathers chicks
28 "We will go with our young and our __" (Ex. 10:9 NIV)
29 Manna measurement
31 Cut off
34 Jesus sermon site
37 Hebrews' oppressor
39 Ethereal
40 "If God be __ us..." (Rom. 8:31)
41 Realm
42 Satanic underling
44 Synagogue opposed Paul (Acts 6:9)
47 Israel crossed on __ land
48 Paul's ports of call
50 __ Lanka
51 __ Sea
52 Promised Land
56 God's nightly pillar
59 "Hide me under the __ of thy wings" (Ps. 17:8)
63 Fourth plague (sing.)
64 Many Bible peoples
66 Computer game player
67 Last Supper's Upper __
68 Banquet invitees' hangout
69 Tithing herb
70 Get ready
71 Lame man's strengthened
72 "I will __ over you" (Ex. 12:13)
73 Wicked ensnared by this

DOWN

1 Texas battle site
2 With 61 down, Bible lands
3 Food from heaven
4 Copper smelted from
5 "Truth which __ with godliness" (Titus 1:1 NKJV)
6 Cat's "motor"
7 Historical time periods
8 Greek tribal land
9 Red Sea tidal action
10 Moses' brother
11 Moses __ up with Pharaoh
12 Samuel to Eli (1 Sam. 2:20)
13 Preach Gospel to the __ of the earth
21 Robe's top
22 Pronoun for Miriam
25 Capital of Japan
27 KJV "before"
29 Offerings' are sweet
30 "What can __ mortals do to me?" (Ps. 118:6 NIV)
31 Psalmist's instrument of praise
32 "That thine eyes may be __ open" (1 Kings 8:29)
33 School org.
34 Lecher's look
35 Pharaoh's pursued Hebrews
36 Chancy

38 Street urchin
39 "__ to your faith virtue" (2 Peter 1:5)
43 Mount Sinai to Edom (dir.)
45 King's guards
46 "__ nigh to God" (James 4:8)
49 Internet pop-ups
51 "__ not ye against the Lord" (Num. 14:9)
53 "Promised __ by his prophets" (Rom. 1:2)
54 Plants of Numbers 24:6
55 Dryad
56 FDR's dog
57 Modern-day enemy of Israel
58 Ephraim army group
60 Camel's water-holder
61 See 2 Down

62 Beasts' homes
65 Marah to Elim dir.
67 LP speed

63

JOSHUA

ACROSS

1 "Every place [you] tread __, that have I given unto you" (Josh. 1:3)
5 Special case only (2 words)
10 Concord, e.g.
13 Harshness, as Exodus 1:13 NKJV
15 Doctrine
16 Pacific battle: __ Jima
17 "__ him with all your heart and...soul" (Josh. 22:5)
18 Eastern religion
19 Promised Land boundary
20 "These stones __ to be a memorial" (Josh. 4:7 NIV)
21 Joshua's tent "door"
23 How Joshua's army traveled
25 Beloved apostle (Sp.)
26 Rahab's cord color
28 Graven image (syn.)
31 Jordan River was at flood __
32 Pain reliever brand
33 Coat
34 Partnership type (Abbr.)
37 Slave transaction
38 Israel's night guide (2 words)
40 "The testimony of the Lord is _" (Ps. 19:7)
41 Int. opposite
42 The Lord sets prisoners __
43 One of 31 Down
44 Also known as
45 Bread-making grain
46 Hold back KJV-style
49 Actor Brad __
50 Deceivers, as Revelation 3:9 NIV
51 Indonesian island
52 Neon or argon
55 First letter of Leviticus
56 Land of milk and __
59 Hebrews came out from
61 Slippery ocean-dweller
62 Evade, as Job 11:20 NIV
63 Israel's northern enemy
64 "Test me, Lord, and __ me" (Ps. 26:2 NIV)
65 Thick
66 Balak's land

DOWN

1 __ Minor (Little Dipper)
2 Jonah's boarding site, maybe
3 Giant
4 All Saint's Day mo.
5 His sin caused Ai defeat
6 Overflow, as Proverbs 5:3 NIV
7 Chick's mom
8 Even's opposite
9 "Be strong and of a good __" (Josh. 1:6)
10 Rahab's rope material, maybe
11 Swedish citizen
12 Crisped bread
14 Joshua created cities of __
22 "__ up his words in thine heart" (Job 22:22)
24 Silver or iron
25 Swing
26 Magis' light
27 Amorites' hiding place
28 "His soul shall dwell at __" (Ps. 25:13)
29 Spy covering (Josh. 2:6)
30 Soft cloth
31 Joshua sent twelve to Canaan
34 Calm down

35 Deborah's location: palm __
36 Financial obligation
38 Tenor's solo
39 Israel's God inspired this
40 Elisha's water healer
   (2 Kings 2:20)
42 Dry bones, post-prophecy
43 Jericho, Ai, e.g.
44 Edited (Abbr.)
45 Cubic centimeter
46 Solomon's ships
47 Cargo vessel
48 Gather, as Isaiah 11:10 NIV
49 Recipient
51 Sleeping places
52 Rotating mechanism
53 Capital of Western Samoa
54 Knife action

57 Bullfight exclamation (Sp.)
58 Joshua's father
60 Workout place

64

THE TWELVE TRIBES

ACROSS

1 French "not"
4 Father of Dan, Gad, e.g.
9 Daniel, to Romans
14 Naphtali to Dan (dir.)
15 Give off
16 Smelly vegetable
17 Strange
18 Crop-destroying weather
19 Eyed
20 "He is thy __, and he is thy God" (Deut. 10:21)
22 Canaan: Israel's new __
24 Pharaoh __ the people go
25 Thieves' hideout (2 words)
27 Trick, as Joshua 9:4 NIV
31 Water pitcher
32 Quick-witted
33 Last Bible book (Abbr.)
34 Quaking tree
36 Judgment comes "as swift as the __" (Deut. 28:49)
38 Candies
40 Elijah's victory site
42 Violin's cousin
43 British county
44 "Let __ the earth fear the LORD" (Ps. 33: 8)
45 Describes road to destruction
47 Mother of six tribes
51 Meat alternative
53 Hannah __ Samuel to God
54 Andean empire
55 Pocket bread
57 Respite
59 Speed
62 Unclean animal (Fr.)
65 Unclean rodent
66 Resource
67 Offering type
68 Israelites __ manna
69 Small bright fish
70 Distance measurements
71 Writer's tool

DOWN

1 Israel, God's chosen __
2 Philip's brother
3 Staid
4 David's dad, for short
5 Cart part
6 Remind
7 Poem
8 Jacob dream site
9 Judgment, as Job 21:30 NKJV
10 Simeon and Levi condemned for (Gen. 49:7)
11 Goose egg
12 Anointed part
13 "I am…the beginning and the __" (Rev. 1:8 NKJV)
21 Twelve tribes of __
23 The Lord our God is __
25 Gets older
26 Cacophony, as Jeremiah 51:55 NIV
28 Exhort
29 Transact business
30 Adam's wife
32 Able
35 Red __
36 Stray, as Psalm 95:10
37 Pilot Earhart
38 Granary
39 Animal describing Benjamin (Gen. 49:27)
40 Gab

41 Assist
42 Wine holder
43 Issachar to Jacob
45 Deli order, for short
46 Property
48 Snare
49 Pointed
50 Hurry, KJV-style
52 The __ Room
56 Small particle
57 Roe's mate
58 Used to make 59 Down
59 Body art, for short
60 Naphtali to Manasseh (dir.)
61 Santa Fe time zone (Abbr.)
63 Mocker's exclamation
64 Golf score

65

THE TABERNACLE

ACROSS

1 Bethel to Mizpah (dir.)
4 Ascend
9 Upset
14 Downwind
15 Relating to the moon
16 Vice __
17 "Take, __: this is my body"
   (1 Cor. 11:24)
18 West African capital
19 Vexed
20 Cluttered
22 Solomon's sailed Red Sea
24 "I led them…with __ of love"
   (Hos. 11:4 NIV)
25 Bridge support
27 Passover sacrifice
31 Sir (Ger.)
32 Nebraska city
33 Hair styler
34 Moses' brother
36 Cursed in Malachi 1:14 NIV
38 *The Matrix* actor Keanu
40 Tabernacle overseer
42 It held shoebread
43 "It is mine to avenge; I will __"
   (Deut. 32:35 NIV)
44 Planet Earth (poet.)
45 Gulf
47 Palm fruit
51 42 Across (Sp.)
53 Real estate document (Abbr.)
54 Sanctuary or courtyard
55 11 Down covering
57 Forbidden temple activity
59 Sacrifice place
62 Fights
65 It stood still for Joshua (Lat.)

66 Position
67 Pursue, as 1 Peter 3:11
68 Before, KJV-style
69 Kinds
70 Written down
71 Concorde, e.g. (Abbr.)

DOWN

1 Caleb was one
2 Tiny hat
3 More damp
4 Dressed
5 Charlie Brown's nemesis
6 Business abbreviation
7 Damage
8 Lampstand part
9 Tel __
10 Ephod gem
11 __ of the covenant
12 Syria to Israel (dir.)
13 Owned
21 God's chosen people
23 Expression of surprise
25 OT prophet
26 How Elijah got to Jezreel
28 Gets older
29 Burnt offering
30 Deli sandwich, for short
32 It's refined by fire
35 Fifth or Madison (Abbr.)
36 U.S. spy grp.
37 Successful period
38 29 Down cooking style
39 Flows' opposite
40 Picnic ant, perhaps
41 LP speed
42 Actor Hanks
43 Really cool

45 Baseball's Ripken
46 "I have __ your word in my heart" (Ps. 119:11)
48 Comes up, as Job 30:12 NKJV
49 Psalm-singing voices
50 Isaiah 40:31 offspring
52 See 10 Down
56 Silver and gold, e.g.
57 Priest's garment color
58 Secondhand
59 Play a role
60 "__ up for yourselves treasures in heaven" (Matt. 6:20)
61 Cooking meas.
63 Spanish "one"
64 NYC time zone

66

THE TEN COMMANDMENTS

ACROSS

1 10 Commandments: __ law
5 Summary
10 Notes that follow mi
13 Filipino dish
15 God's highest "law" (Fr.)
16 "__ my people go" (Ex. 5:1)
17 Commandment receiver
18 Mushrooms
19 Copper made from this
20 Before, as Exodus 1:19
21 Domestic friends
23 Teacher's role (Eph. 4:12 NIV)
25 Epochs
26 Covers
28 Country separator
31 Greek philosopher
32 Lamenting poetry
33 Charity
34 Typing speed (Abbr.)
37 Actor Hackman
38 Do not bear __ witness
40 Roman church "Good-bye" from
41 Boiled, as 2 Chronicles 35:13
42 Surrender
43 Book of Numbers purpose
44 Offering site
45 "I bore you on __ wings"
   (Ex. 19:4 NKJV)
46 More terrifying
49 Keep the Sabbath day __
50 Same, as Deuteronomy 1:17 NIV
51 Fallen
52 Average work performance
55 Land east of Eden
56 Doves' homes
59 Make no graven __

61 Day after Mon.
62 Kinds
63 Comforts
64 "... __ to your faith virtue"
   (2 Peter 1:5 NKJV)
65 Sordid
66 Blood placed on a door __

DOWN

1 Esau hunted this
2 Aroma
3 Medicine amount
4 Marah to Elim (dir.)
5 Nile floaters
6 Australian birds
7 Prisoner, slangily
8 Mo. before Sept.
9 God's people: a kingdom of __
10 Unleavened bread ingredient
11 45 Across home (var.)
12 "A man's __ are of the Lord"
   (Prov. 20:24 NKJV)
14 Hawk
22 Listen, give __
24 Status __
25 Hebrews camped on __ of the
   wilderness
26 Evils
27 Don't take the Lord's __ in vain
28 Pleads
29 Fake butter
30 "A time to __, and a time to sew"
   (Eccl. 3:7)
31 Whiter
34 You shall not __
35 Revelation horse named Death
36 Heavy barges

38 Esther's banquet (Fr.)
39 Sixth month (Jewish calendar)
40 Wary
42 Customers
43 Walkie-__
44 __ of the Covenant
45 Long time
46 Christmas man
47 Hebrews led by this
48 Helped
49 Saucy girl
51 Lampstand part
52 El __, Texas
53 Gets older
54 Sabbath activity

57 Keep the law "as the apple of thine __" (Prov. 7:2)
58 Resort hotel
60 Joshua's men made one

67

JUDGES

ACROSS

1 Jael, __ of 48 Down
5 Caught with a lasso
10 Leah was Rachel's, for short
13 Burst out
15 Wedding walkway
16 Dynamite (Abbr.)
17 Canaanite city
18 How vines grow
19 "Long, long __"
20 Tyre to Sidon (dir.)
21 "The Israelites did evil in the __ of the Lord" (Judges 2:11 NIV)
23 Fire appeared __ of Mount Sinai (2 words)
25 Prod
26 Lunges
28 Israel would do to enemies
31 Psalm
32 Humor
33 Boaz's kin
34 The anger of the Lord was __ against Israel
37 __ of Solomon
38 Said, KJV-style
40 Tropical edible root
41 Sensory info conductor (Abbr.)
42 "He shall __ his people from their sins" (Matt. 1:21)
43 OT measurement
44 Protection
45 Mr. Mandela
46 First judge
49 Aramaic Father
50 Stalks
51 Left by boil or burn
52 Israel's enemy, in general
55 Eve's beginning

56 He hid idols, Judges 17:5
59 "The Lord __ the eyes of the blind" (Ps. 146:8 NKJV)
61 Samson __ honey
62 Wroth
63 African-American grp.
64 Pronoun for Deborah
65 Roman goddess
66 Tiny ark flyer

DOWN

1 Gaal saw shadows, "as if they __ men" (Judg. 9:36)
2 Modern name for Xerxes's land
3 Be angry
4 Nature conservation grp.
5 Had a speed contest
6 Anointing liquids
7 Greek twenty-third letter
8 Shade tree
9 Fourth judge
10 RBI, ERA, e.g.
11 Block of metal
12 Ceases, as Job 18:5 NIV
14 Athens debate topic
22 Sweet potato
24 Joshua's father
25 Group of criminals
26 Like a bow string
27 Hebrew eighth letter
28 Record
29 Chariot metal
30 Anak had three (Judg. 1:20)
31 Uses a lever
34 Belonging to Noah's son
35 Brand of sandwich cookie
36 Unclean items must be __ out
38 Cooking herb

39 Antihistamine
40 Issachar son
42 Caused by earthquake
43 Land given to Caleb
44 Whichever
45 Pro sports grp.
46 Ms. Winfrey
47 Corny
48 His wife killed Sisera
49 Heart sometimes does this
51 Fill
52 Israel's God inspired this
53 __ upon a time
54 Sports channel
57 God's wrath
58 Wheeled vehicle
60 Lion's foot

68

GIDEON

ACROSS

1 "Blessed __ the merciful" (Matt. 5:3)
4 Israel dwelt __ their enemies
9 Excretes
14 Trap, as in Job 18:9
15 Title for Jesus
16 Sleep disorder
17 "Blessed are those who __ justly" (Ps. 106:3 NIV)
18 "The children of Israel __ unto the Lord" (Judg. 6:6)
19 "Let your eyes look straight __" (Prov. 4:25 NIV)
20 Breeches cover these
22 European monetary unit
24 Frau's husband
25 Courts
27 Israel's hideouts (Judg. 6:2)
31 "Before the throne there was __ of glass" (2 words) (Rev. 4:6)
32 Bread the Lord provided
33 32 Across creation, perhaps
34 Gideon's altar called The Lord Is __ (Judg. 6:24 NIV)
36 King's ruling
38 Homes to Leviathan
40 Gideon's test of God's will
42 Light appeared this creation day
43 Knobs
44 Crimson Tide state (Abbr.)
45 Norway waterway
47 Thought
51 In __ (together)
53 Slime
54 Gideon's reward
55 "Without counsel, plans go __" (Prov. 15:22 NKJV)

57 Uzziah was __ from the temple (2 Chron. 26:21 NIV)
59 Sri __
62 Eyed
65 Roman greeting (Lat.)
66 Saul's right-hand man
67 "__ my heart to fear thy name" (Ps. 86:11)
68 Number of servants Gideon had
69 Wine or oil maker
70 Egypt's southern neighbor
71 Miracle part of angel's staff

DOWN

1 Miss Marples creator Christie
2 What Solomon got with wisdom
3 Whole, as in Acts 18:8 NIV
4 Roman doorway
5 Paul spoke on __ Hill
6 Kimono sash
7 Jezreel to Endor (dir.)
8 His name means "Mighty Warrior"
9 France and Germany river
10 Priest's garment
11 Bethel to Shiloh dir.
12 Pod vegetable
13 Nehemiah's emotion
21 Israel harvest
23 Springsteen's "Born in the __"
25 Female WWII units
26 "Love __ another" (John 13:34)
28 Heroic
29 French resort town
30 Tennis match part
32 Gideon, e.g.
35 Last Supper purpose
36 Unclean seafood

37 Decorative pattern
38 Fatty
39 Ocean Spray's drink starters
40 It consumed Gideon's offering
41 Ishmael, Isaac, e.g.
42 Musical tones
43 Group of apostles (Abbr.)
45 "If God be __ us...?"(Rom. 8:31)
46 Blissful, as Est. 8:15 NIV
48 Give a contribution
49 Disciples minus Judas
50 Subtrahend opposite
52 Gideon's offering
56 David fought many
57 Second letter in Thessalonica
58 Yemen gulf
59 How Gideon's men must drink
60 Abridged (Abbr.)
61 Tyre to Sidon dir.
63 African antelope
64 Chest top

69

SAMSON

ACROSS

1 Pop-ups
4 Samson's birthplace
9 "__with your adversary quickly" (Matt. 5:25 NKJV)
14 Hind's mate
15 Alpha and __
16 Potato side dish
17 "To bind Samson __ we come up" (Judg. 15:10)
18 "I will __ leave thee, nor forsake thee" (Heb. 13:5)
19 Raised line
20 Philistines to Israel (2 words)
22 Samson slew one
24 Notion
25 "Will you keep to the old path that the wicked have ___?" (Job 22:15 NIV)
27 Gideon's fleece condition
31 Crop Samson destroyed
32 Fast walks
33 Contend with
34 Eyed
36 Mock attack
38 Samson pre-marriage role
40 Samson wedding game
42 Ladies' covering
43 Capacitor measure
44 Before, KJV-style
45 "Beat your...pruning __ into spears" (Joel 3:10 NIV)
47 Wading bird
51 Samson sleeps here (pl.)
53 David's weapon (Fr.)
54 Samson's wife threat: "or __"
55 To be, past tense
57 Solomon was __ of all men

59 "You will not let your holy one see __" (Acts 2:27 NIV)
62 Samson holders
65 Squirrel's find
66 Accustomed to
67 Hearing-related
68 Remove (Abbr.)
69 Beginnings
70 Stir up
71 Shiloh to Jericho (dir.)

DOWN

1 Egypt's language
2 City of gold, El __
3 Sower
4 Area
5 Sign
6 John's vision (Abbr.)
7 Life stage
8 Delilah's profession
9 Hairstyle
10 Samson's labor
11 Divest
12 Brain wave detector (Abbr.)
13 Sidon to Hazor (dir.)
21 Samson's father
23 Name tags, e.g.
25 Terebinth or fig
26 Shepherd's tool
28 Israelites' behavior, many times
29 Forbidden for Nazarite
30 Still
32 Educational channel (Abbr.)
35 Ark-dwelling antelope
36 Prescription regulator (Abbr.)
37 Jordan whirlpools
38 Samson's tool for 31 Across
39 Tea type

40 Eden tool
41 Taxing agency (Abbr.)
42 Valentine mo.
43 Rival
45 Pronoun for Delilah
46 Musical productions
48 Mixes
49 Releases
50 Clinch
52 Bee group
56 Samson's were put out
57 Samson post-haircut condition
58 Cyprus is one
59 Use a shovel
60 Tyre to Sidon (dir.)
61 Mangy dog
63 Enemies were driven __ of the
   Promised Land
64 Con's opposite

70

OLD TESTAMENT KINGS

ACROSS

1 Chinese seasoning (Abbr.)
4 Mansion
9 Offering residue
14 U.S. Gulf state (Abbr.)
15 Software
16 Laugher on the ark
17 Taste and __ that the Lord is good
18 Man after God's own heart
19 State of king's military
20 King's assistant
22 Mongolian desert
24 27 Across this type of king
25 Always
27 Son of Manasseh
31 Ten (Prefix)
32 Mortar, as Genesis 11:3
33 Org. concerned with energy
34 Not expensive, like sparrows
36 Arose (2 words)
38 Rift
40 Roe and hind playgrounds
42 Visitor
43 Pressed oil
44 Good king of Judah
45 Son of Jeroboam
47 Caesar was king here
51 Defunct monetary unit
53 Israel refused this command
54 Prophet during Uzziah's reign
55 Commander and king
57 Saul pursued David here
59 Bitty
62 Son of 9 Down
65 Jeans maker
66 "We eagerly __ a Savior…" (Phil. 3:20 NIV)
67 Trumpet sound
68 Hebron to Masada (dir.)
69 Bird's seat
70 Vineyard blossoms (Song 1:14 NIV)
71 Doubting disciple, to friends

DOWN

1 Sixties dance, __ Potato
2 King's robe part
3 Celtic language
4 Fixed
5 Sixth Jewish calendar month
6 Veterans Day mo.
7 __-Wan Kenobi
8 Describes ruby (2 words)
9 Jezebel's husband
10 Israel's adversary
11 Jesus' healed (Matt. 9:20)
12 Judah to Aram (dir.)
13 Nehemiah emotion
21 Sacrifice sites: high __
23 Unrefined metal
25 David v. Goliath site
26 King descriptor (Abbr.)
28 Dole out
29 Musical composition
30 Snooze
32 NYSE oversight grp.
35 Beret
36 Joseph role (Abbr.)
37 Some 29 Down
38 Occupied
39 Valid
40 Kill
41 __ of Congress (Abbr.)
42 Helium or radon
43 Poem

45 Neither's partner
46 Wicked king of Judah
48 Breakfast egg
49 Overly (2 words)
50 "Let each __ others better than themselves" (Phil. 2:3)
52 Doric alternative
56 Skeptic's opinion of Flood
57 Repair socks
58 Jane Austen heroine
59 Type of dance
60 Ram's mate
61 Serving of corn
63 Bullfight exclamation
64 How deserters fled

71

DAVID

ACROSS

1 Captains housed in them
6 Esau served Isaac this
10 Priests' headwear
14 Bathsheba's husband
15 Offering made three times a __
16 U.S. canal
17 David did before the ark
18 Amount, as Exodus 16:4
19 Joshua to Moses
20 Deer relative
21 Certain disciple, to friends
23 Gideon's fleece
25 Mets' former home
26 Number of Eli's sons
27 One who sups
30 In abundance
34 David cast aside Saul's
35 Double-reed instrument
36 David did with arrow
38 "A very large __ ...assembled in Jerusalem" (2 Chron. 30:13 NIV)
39 Gaza to Bethlehem (dir.)
40 Gem carved in relief
42 David's horse food
43 Lampstand center
44 Elongated circles
45 Israel council member
48 Lyre sounds, maybe
49 "Make man in __ image" (Gen. 1:26)
50 Spy order, "__ the land" (Josh. 2:1)
51 Very dark blue
54 David killed one
55 Boaz to Ruth
58 Sticky black substances
59 Daniel's mind (Dan. 5:12 NIV)

61 Eat away
63 David's weapon (Fr.)
64 Soul singer Franklin
65 Voids
66 U.K. stables
67 "Set me as a __ upon thine heart" (Song 8:6)
68 Doctrine

DOWN

1 Love is not __
2 Israel's history, at first
3 Mark 5:11 sound
4 Apple computer
5 David's boyhood role
6 David put garrisons there
7 Bluish green
8 Jonathan refused to do this
9 "We __ not against flesh and blood" (Eph. 6:12)
10 Direct confrontation (2 words)
11 Describes wilderness
12 Jonah sailed on it
13 "Mine eyes have __ thy salvation" (Luke 2:30)
22 Pronoun for Abigail
24 "__ no man any thing" (Rom. 13:8)
25 Store
27 Mexican sandwich
28 Tapestry
29 Moses did to rock twice
30 Saul's captain (2 Sam. 2:8)
31 Psalm, e.g.
32 Amnon's sister
33 "__ yourselves unto the Lord" (2 Chron. 30:8)

35 Jesus went up __ a mountain to pray
37 Model Kate
40 Focused
41 Hannah made one (2 words)
43 "A fool's lips...calleth for __" (Prov. 18:6)
46 Heard with thunder in Revelation 8:5
47 Eighth month (Abbr.)
48 Spy org.
50 Corrupt
51 Object
52 Back of neck
53 Peter __ his sword
54 High place (Heb.)
55 Rhine university city (Gr.)
56 Overseer called Hebrews
57 Eagle's home

60 Before, KJV-style
62 Bible herb

72

SOLOMON

ACROSS

1 Joab __ Abner
5 Large gathering
10 NT epistle (Abbr.)
13 Wreak __
15 Circle measurements
16 Toreador's shout
17 Type of acid
18 Solomon's bread cookers
19 Shoshonean
20 Hair stuff
21 Solomon's mind
23 Temple wood
25 Jordan River __ and flows
26 Complete
28 Solomon's request of God
31 Cities Solomon built
   (1 Kings 9:19)
32 38 Across metal type
33 Angels sat "where the body of
   Jesus had __" (John 20:12)
34 Sidon to Tyre (dir.)
37 NBA's __ dunk
38 Temple metal
40 Unconsciousness state
41 Los Angeles time zone
42 Southeast Asia country
43 "The __ filled the temple…"
   (1 Kings 8:10 NIV)
44 Solomon's kingdom
45 Repetitive singing
46 Vegetable cooker
49 Imitated
50 Bird speech
51 Burn
52 Back of the boat
55 Solomon "got __ of all the
   idols…" (1 Kings 15:12 NIV)

56 Distribute
59 Open sore
61 Holy __ of Israel
62 Solomon's visitor
63 Donkey
64 Scandinavian currency (Abbr.)
65 How 23 Across were harvested
66 Solomon, e.g. (slang)

DOWN

1 Thick carpet
2 Mephibosheth's condition
3 Good's opposite
4 David "__over the hearts of the
   men of Judah" (2 Sam. 19:14 NIV)
5 "The message of the __ is foolish-
   ness" (1 Cor. 1:18)
6 Praise enthusiastically
7 Lyric poem
8 Gain, as Proverbs 3:4 NIV
9 "That I may __ between good…"
   (1 Kings 3:9 NKJV)
10 Dutch cheese
11 Adonijah refuge site
12 Untrusting
14 Herder
22 Large computer co.
24 Edom to Moab (dir.)
25 Israel's enemy
26 Educational groups (Abbr.)
27 Timothy's grandmother
28 Bee's cousin
29 Iniquities
30 Strip
31 Sword action
34 Jesus said, "I am coming __"
35 Obscenity
36 Bunches

38 Told, KJV-style
39 Lion's exclamation
40 Dressed
42 Chunky
43 Mercy seat angel
44 It held manna
45 April 15 guy (Abbr.)
46 Prepared young fish
47 "__ upon me, my God, for good" (Neh. 5:19)
48 Bedspread feather
49 "Let your eyes look straight __" (Prov. 4:25 NIV)
51 Ice piece
52 Land measurement
53 Day 3 creation, perhaps
54 Horse's gait

57 Pronoun for 62 Across
58 Create a garment
60 Tote

73

SAMUEL

ACROSS

1 Revelation sea critter
6 Samuel's firstborn
10 5th NT book
14 __ and Omega
15 Job 9:9 NIV constellation (Lat.)
16 Epistle recipient, to friends
17 Foreign-born
18 __ of Agriculture (Abbr.)
19 Mound
20 Hart's jump
21 Time past
22 Samuel's was __ by God
24 Samuel before Israel: " __ I am!"
   (1 Sam. 12:3)
26 Tears
27 __ from the body, present with
   the Lord
30 Samuel role
31 "Hannah was praying in her __"
   (1 Sam. 1:13 NIV)
32 Use a divining rod
33 Hannah and Elkanah state
36 Practice piece
37 "Hannah, why __ you weeping?
   (1 Sam. 1:8 NIV)
38 Advance (arch.)
40 OT prophet (Abbr.)
41 Walked, as Ezekiel 19:6 NKJV
43 Indian dwelling
44 Wading bird
45 Female parent
46 Stephen's fate
49 Put away foreign __
50 Goat type
51 Some
52 Demons
56 Jeremiah's abode, at times
57 Modern-day Persia
59 Cuddly Aussie
60 Reed instrument
61 French resort town
62 Block of silver
63 Scepter
64 Pride __ before destruction
65 "Yet turn not __ from following
   the Lord" (1 Sam. 12:20)

DOWN

1 False god
2 Pronoun for Hannah (Fr.)
3 Capital of Western Samoa
4 David's pre-king role
5 Beige
6 Early role for Samuel
7 Favorite dipping cookie
8 Sixth sense (Abbr.)
9 Door fastener (pl.)
10 "Keep me as the __ of the eye"
   (Ps. 17:8)
11 Samuel lent to God as a __
12 Roof materials
13 Sliding toy
21 Are, KJV-style
23 Jesus __ in Gethsemane
25 Door, KJV-style
26 Dorcas did this
27 "Excuse me!"
28 Second letter in Corinth
29 Samuel anointed him
30 Job had many
32 Shepherd king
33 Hannah __ before the Lord
34 Dueling sword
35 Elk's cousin
39 Stresses

1	2	3	4	5		6	7	8	9		10	11	12	13
14						15					16			
17						18					19			
20					21				22	23				
			24	25				26						
27	28	29					30							
31					32					33	34	35	
36					37				38	39			
40				41	42				43				
			44				45						
	46	47	48				49						
50					51				52	53	54	55	
56				57	58			59				
60				61				62				
63				64				65				

42 Doing what you're told
45 Swear
46 Solomon's visitor's home
47 Eagle's claw
48 Eyed
49 Bodily makeup
50 Flat-bottomed boat
51 Dagon found fallen on his
53 Manger visitors
54 Slog
55 Gorge, as Proverbs 23:20 NIV
58 Euphrates, e.g. (Sp.)
59 Car maker

74

SAMUEL

ACROSS

1 It won't wash away sin
5 Boat type
10 Jezebel or Ahab, e.g. (Abbr.)
13 French region
15 God to Elijah: "I will send rain upon the __" (1 Kings 18:1)
16 Holy __ of Israel
17 "The __ of your guilt is still before me" (Jer. 2:22 NIV)
18 God to Job: "__ yourself like a man (Job 38:3 NIV)
19 God's breath result (Job 37:10)
20 Boston's are red
21 Temple sacrifice activity
23 Repeat
25 Thessalonian cheese
26 Dive types
28 Shortage in Elijah's time
31 Beast of Jude 10
32 Wield
33 Boaz's love
34 Unclean meat
37 Pronoun for Jezebel (Fr.)
38 Spanish seasoning
40 Gooey cake
41 Be holy, __ apart
42 Oil type
43 Elijah poured on sacrifice
44 Taken __
45 Ark dwellers
46 Exceed in status
49 Widow's cake ingredient
50 Rachel's pre-Jacob state
51 Cincinnati baseball team
52 Nathanael's tree (John 1:48)
55 __ Chi
56 Jacob's father

59 Elicit
61 Gray sea eagle
62 Elijah miracle site (1 Kings 17:19) (syn.)
63 Tree of Eden, perhaps
64 Pumpernickel
65 Ark giggler
66 Elijah "__ and dwelt by…" (1 Kings 17:5)

DOWN

1 Talk back
2 "Follow __ know the Lord" (Hosea 6:3) (2 words)
3 Trojan War hero
4 Luau dish
5 Striped ark dweller
6 Garner
7 Undergarment
8 And so forth (Abbr.)
9 66 Across site
10 God's was still, small
11 Acquire, as Exodus 28:43 NIV
12 David and Jonathan
14 Straight
22 Colorado native
24 Mount Carmel to Galilee (dir.)
25 God's answer on Mount Carmel
26 Food (slang)
27 Manual opposite
28 Charges
29 Chariot part
30 Heat result
31 Elijah eating place
34 Unclean rodents
35 To incite
36 Israel fought many
38 Actor Rickman

39 Decorate, as Jeremiah 10:4
40 False prophets followed him
42 Ahab helper
43 Otter's cousin
44 Blessed __ the merciful
45 Dreams and visions site
46 Cherubim site, __ court
   (Ezek. 10:5)
47 Single
48 Sheaf holder, perhaps
49 Saudi city
51 Elijah prayed for it
52 Be angry
53 Computer picture button
54 Fellow, for short
57 Prodigal Son dwelling
58 Elijah did at Zarephath
60 Gideon's fleece covering

ACROSS

1 Joseph dream symbol
6 Satan's minions
10 Elisha to widow: "__ the oil, and pay" (2 Kings 4:7)
14 Elisha to Elijah: "I will not __ thee" (2 Kings 2:2)
15 Space agcy.
16 __ 51
17 Weapon of deliverance
18 Days __ by, according to Job 9:25
19 Jacob and Joseph (slang)
20 __ Hai
21 "In my flesh shall I __ God" (Job 19:26)
22 Stage whispers
24 Widow's oil paid hers
26 Less refined
27 How army marches (2 words)
30 30 Down, British var.
31 "Chariots of fire __ about Elisha" (2 Kings 6:17)
32 Outside of city limits, as Esther 9:19 NIV
33 __ forma
36 Income opposite
37 Widow's filled every jar
38 Expression
40 Gilgal to Shiloh (dir.)
41 Controls for Naaman's horses
43 Loon-like seabird
44 Elisha used to cure waters
45 "I have __ thy precepts" (Ps. 119:173)
46 Raven does to Elijah
49 Highway transport
50 Elisha's pottage poison
51 London time zone (Abbr.)
52 Prodigal's meal (Luke 15:16 NIV)
56 Tribe's land measurement
57 Drag, as in Luke 12:58
59 Leah to Rachel
60 Chariot puller, perhaps
61 Elisha's sacrifice
62 Silly
63 Elisha's head
64 Adam's garden job
65 Stared

DOWN

1 High place part
2 Goddess at Corinth
3 British nobleman
4 "__ profane and vain babblings" (1 Tim. 6:20)
5 Elisha: "Borrow not a __ " (2 Kings 4:3)
6 Inserted graphic
7 Elijah to widow: "__ me...a little cake" (1 Kings 17:13)
8 Philippian letter
9 Elisha prophesied here
10 Jacob's food descriptor (syn.)
11 Wear away
12 Naaman's fate
13 She helped Naaman
21 Samaria to Shechem (dir.)
23 "So the __ went back the ten steps" (Isa. 38:8 NIV)
25 Elijah's mantle did this for Elisha
26 Bicep exercises
27 Elisha made this swim
28 Part of speech
29 Psalmist instrument
30 One of five, for short

32 Churns
33 Blackbird desserts
34 David sliced Saul's
35 Portent
39 Sagging
42 Within the sound of voice
45 Grass's fate
46 Hot beverage
47 Relating to the ear
48 Fad
49 Correct
50 Ephod was priest's (slang)
51 Megiddo or Hinnom (var.)
53 __ Office
54 Great canine
55 Winter transport
58 27 Down swimmer
59 Jordan, et. al. (Sp.)

76

MAJOR PROPHETS

ACROSS

1 Manasseh's tribe size
5 "Make __ to help me, O Lord" (Ps. 38:22)
10 Flight control (Abbr.)
13 Elude
15 Abraham's son
16 Neither's partner
17 Island nation
18 Kislev month number
19 __ of the Lord
20 Ram's mate
21 Nothing
23 Makes money
25 Satan, father of these, slangily
26 Goliath, compared to others
28 Assents to
31 36 Down's home
32 Porridge
33 Elijah's prayer-brought liquid
34 Resort hotel
37 Throw out
38 Boat's back end
40 Dregs, as Ezekiel 24:11
41 Samaria to Damascus (dir.)
42 Belonging to Miriam
43 Car rental firm
44 Those of Ezekiel's prophecy were dry
45 Fauna's kin
46 Clash
49 Cain __ Abel
50 Gives off
51 "I will __ out my wrath on you" (Ezek. 21:31 NIV)
52 "Every knee shall __, every tongue shall swear" (Isa. 45:23)
55 14 Down cell

56 Lukewarm
59 Typographic character
61 "Even to your old __ I am he" (Isa. 46:4)
62 Mrs. Peron
63 Winter vehicles
64 Awesome, for short
65 Doesn't own
66 Craving

DOWN

1 "__ the evil, and love the good" (Amos 5:15)
2 Promise
3 "The __ Ranger"
4 Bible land tree
5 "He will make my feet like __ feet..." (Hab. 3:19)
6 Babylon's continent
7 __ Francisco
8 Make lace
9 Level
10 Peter's brother (Fr.)
11 Financial transactions
12 David and Bathsheba event
14 55 Across prophet
22 Core muscles, for short
24 Tuscaloosa state (Abbr.)
25 Beautiful appendages (Isa. 52:7)
26 "A time to __ down...a time to build" (Eccl. 3:3 NIV)
27 Like
28 Conflict
29 Cadge
30 Gibeonites' tactic
31 Lock of Samson's hair
34 Wound result
35 Isaiah 11:6 kin

36 Fig-growing prophet
38 "Here am I; __ me" (Isa. 6:8)
39 Fig Olive or almond, e.g.
40 "The Lord is __ to anger" (Nah. 1:3)
42 Lifting machine
43 Prophecies, perhaps
44 Deli sandwich
45 Ague-like illness
46 Lebanon wood source
47 "I am the Alpha and __" (Rev. 1:8; 1:11)
48 Temple walls __ with cedar
49 Carbonated drinks
51 Brad ___, actor
52 Sky color (Fr.)
53 Chances of winning
54 Horizon direction
57 First woman

58 Attach
60 Jesus healed the __

77

ISAIAH

ACROSS

1 Gas burner
5 Isaiah speech, perhaps (2 words)
10 Priest's headwear
13 "__ is deceptive, and beauty is fleeting" (Prov. 31:30 NIV)
15 Interrogate
16 Helen Keller's "speech" (Abbr.)
17 Island nation
18 Pottage server, perhaps
19 Tax man (Abbr.)
20 "The __ of joy for mourning" (Isa. 61:3)
21 Sins "shall be as white as __" (Isa. 1:18)
23 Silky material
25 Sound, as Jeremiah 4:5
26 "Learn to do right; seek __" (Isa. 1:17 NIV)
28 Goliath "__ the armies of the living God" (1 Sam. 17:36 NIV)
31 Flare
32 Turn over
33 Got on in years
34 Downwind
37 God knows what you __ before you ask Him
38 Board game
40 One touched Isaiah's lips
41 Place, as Isaiah 14:1
42 Hard labor result, perhaps
43 Temple entrances
44 Pacific Island
45 House of God
46 Wormwood (var.)
49 Isaiah's clothing
50 Halley's is one
51 Is not, slangily
52 Metric weight unit
55 Jordan __ (Sp.)
56 Ancient river valley
59 *Phantom of the __*"
61 Antlered ark-dweller
62 40 Across heater (2 words)
63 Agricultural
64 Dan to Megiddo (dir.)
65 "Wash and make yourselves __" (Isa. 1:16 NIV)
66 "The Lord has anointed me to proclaim good __" (Isa. 61:1 NIV)

DOWN

1 Repeated sound
2 Asian citizen
3 One fastened Jesus' hand
4 "How __ thou fallen from heaven" (Isa. 14:12)
5 62 Across byproduct (2 words)
6 Entice, as Isaiah 5:18
7 Ark of the covenant top
8 Sick
9 Consecrated
10 Sinai plants
11 Gelled dish
12 Carpenter's tool, as Isaiah 44:13 NKJV
14 Deceived
22 Cain's second home
24 Fed on
25 "__ up the brokenhearted" (Isa. 61:1)
26 Oil holders
27 Wields
28 Asks repeatedly for payment
29 Fencing sword

30 Beautiful appendages of Isaiah 52:7
31 Matador's passes at bull
34 Intertwine
35 Countess's mate
36 "I am the Lord, and there is none __" (Isa. 45:6)
38 Unable
39 The Lord, __ and exalted
40 "__ now, let us reason together" (Isa. 1:18 ESV)
42 ___ Grand Am
43 28 Down receiver
44 Fasten
45 2,000 pounds
46 Land allotment
47 Job's afflictions
48 Temple filler, as Isaiah 6:4

49 "He is not here: for he is __" (Matt. 28:6)
51 Manner
52 "Stop trusting in __ humans" (Isa. 2:22 NIV)
53 Animal stomach
54 Mary, Martha, e.g., slangily
57 Rams or Patriots org.
58 We must __ to self
60 Play on words

ACROSS

1 Industrial and Victorian
5 Digit doused in offering
10 Brain and spinal cord (Abbr.)
13 Talking bird, often
15 Painting prop
16 Molder
17 South Florida city
18 Woodworker's tool
19 Southern state (Abbr.)
20 "__ to your faith virtue" (2 Peter 1:5)
21 Skullcap
23 Job's tormentor
25 Slide out of control
26 Opposite of Satan's desire (Isa. 14:14)
28 The Good News
31 Nineteenth U.S. president
32 "__ came I out of my mother's womb..." (Job 1:21)
33 "Leah was tender __" (Gen. 29:17)
34 Noah's son
37 Israel's climate
38 It withers and fades
40 Tyre to Damascus (dir.)
41 Cooking meas.
42 "The parched ground shall become a __" (Isa. 35:7)
43 Jacques's hat
44 Flowers' destinies
45 Jerusalem condition
46 Job's comforters
49 Age (var.)
50 Where Satan roams
51 Sports award
52 Gilead to Ammon (dir.)
55 Seventh letter in Corinth
56 Ms. Winfrey
59 "Remember to __ his work" (Job 36:24 NIV)
61 "__ not my enemies triumph over me" (Ps. 25:2 NKJV)
62 Third plague (Sing.)
63 Goddess in Ephesus
64 Moab to Edom (dir.)
65 Inches forward
66 Cyrus's land today

DOWN

1 Actress Thompson
2 Philistine activity
3 Prep school (Abbr.)
4 Prophet, to friends
5 Neither hot nor cold
6 "It will be for a time, times and __ a time" (Dan. 12:7 NIV)
7 North American country
8 Job, Elihu, e.g.
9 "__ be the name of the Lord" (Job 1:21)
10 Large wooden box
11 Pitcher Ryan
12 "My redeemer liveth, and...shall __ at the latter day..."(Job19:25)
14 Opposite of righteous
22 Anointing substance
24 Medical research org. (Abbr.)
25 Rushed
26 Job's friends sat seven __
27 Job sees with these
28 62 Across synonym
29 Job's boat movers
30 Calf's "walk" (Ps. 29:6)

31 "He __ the brokenhearted" (Ps. 147:3 NKJV)
34 Food enhancer
35 Cain's brother
36 Dole out
38 Precious metal
39 Destroys, as Prov. 14:30 NIV
40 Gaza to Hebron (dir.)
42 Puncture, as with a tack
43 Raised one's spirits
44 Job after rain
45 Exercise unit (Abbr.)
46 Senses
47 Fees
48 Aging
49 Job's seat

51 "His soul shall dwell at __" (Ps. 25:13)
52 Name for Satan: morning __
53 __ fide
54 Vivacity
57 Swine food (sing.)
58 Sisera's covering (Judg. 4:18 ASV)
60 Tribes of Israel, in Rome

JEREMIAH

ACROSS

1 Compel, as Luke 12:58
5 Recorded, old school
10 Synapse-stored info (Abbr.)
13 Puccini creation
15 Delight in, as Song 1:4 NIV
16 "His horses __ swifter than eagles" (Jer. 4:13)
17 It's desperately wicked
18 Rose of Sharon part
19 Days Jeremiah waited on God
20 Opposite of even
21 Adolescent
23 Book by Homer
25 Fruit in Jeremiah's vision
26 Learned ones
28 Multicolored cat
31 Jacob's shrank
32 Baking places
33 Can be sweet or foul
34 Dust used in grieving
37 Love "in __ and in truth" (1 John 3:18)
38 Actress Mirren
40 Resist the devil, and he will __ from you
41 __ of the covenant
42 The Lord's is everlasting
43 Friction match
44 North African capital
45 Tree of Jeremiah's prophecy
46 A woman's should be modest
49 Jesus, called Faithful and __
50 Wood that hinders vision (Matt. 7:5 NIV)
51 Yokel
52 The wicked's exclamation

55 God to Jeremiah, "__ not, I am a child" (Jer. 1:7)
56 Tiny island
59 __ duck
61 Samaria to Galilee (dir.)
62 Mount Everest nation
63 "With my God I can __ a wall" (Ps. 18:29 NIV)
64 Bethel to Gath (dir.)
65 Type of literature
66 Statue of Liberty poet Lazarus

DOWN

1 Gen. 21:6 sound (2 words)
2 Copied
3 Fire-consumed metal
4 God's people do this
5 Used for 5 Across
6 Thieves' dwelling (2 words)
7 Jeremiah's boiling vision
8 Time period
9 God, "I am with thee to __ thee" (Jer. 1:8)
10 Silky material
11 Trick or __
12 Repairs
14 Garrets
22 Sense of self
24 "I will put my __ in their...hearts" (Jer. 31:33)
25 "Seek and ye shall __" (Matt. 7:7)
26 "Fear is on every __" (Jer. 49:29)
27 Soon, as Mark 1:30
28 Psalm part
29 Allege
30 Eaten in Egypt
31 Foot bottoms
34 As well as

35 "Eye hath not __, nor ear heard..." (1 Cor. 2:9)
36 Jeremiah warning, "Take __"
38 Sharpen
39 Doing this brings destruction
40 Be mad
42 Lingering, as Psalm 17:12
43 Strokes of luck
44 Light brown
45 Rainbow shape
46 Recesses
47 "I know the __ I have for you" (Jer. 29:11 NIV)
48 Recipient
49 Jesus' was "King of the Jews"
51 Shema, "__, O Israel..."
52 Eden dweller
53 Ship's steering mechanism
54 Region

57 "O taste and __ that the Lord is good" (Ps. 34:8)
58 Healthcare worker (Abbr.)
60 Frozen water

80

DANIEL

ACROSS

1 Washes
6 Son of Aram (Gen. 10:23)
10 Goddess in Ephesus
14 Lion's mouth closer
15 Daniel's sole beverage (Sp.)
16 Nebuchadnezzar ate like these
17 Describes Revelation visions
18 Legal claim
19 "Jacob was a __ man"
   (Gen. 25:27 NKJV)
20 "I will put enmity between…
   your offspring and ___"
   (Gen. 3:15 NIV)
21 __ Francisco, CA
22 Some are sweet
24 Yucky
26 Timid
27 Hunting expedition
30 Where handwriting appeared
31 Some early Christians died in one
32 "Your heart will __ …with joy"
   (Isa. 60:5 NIV)
33 Resort hotel
36 Belshazzar hosted one
37 Pronoun for Nebuchadnezzar
38 Moral principle
40 Daniel prayed, "O my God,
   incline thine __" (Dan. 9:18)
41 Daniel's vision, "tree in the
   midst of the __" (Dan. 4:10)
43 Name meaning shepherd
44 Lot was to __ Sodom
45 Tabernacle décor
46 Compartment
49 Daniel diet test lasted ten __
50 Glumly
51 Daniel thrown in lions'

52 Job's skin did this
56 *Les Miz's* Hathaway
57 Golden calf
59 Produce or dairy, often
60 Student org.
61 One of Columbus's ships
62 Regress
63 A rod from the __ of Jesse
64 Beauty of old men: __ hair
65 Tabernacle part: __ court

DOWN

1 Priest's belt
2 Sacrifice made __ a year
3 Another name for Sinai
4 Cyrus and others
5 Sneaky
6 Southeast Asia peninsula
7 Opposite of fer (slang)
8 "If any man will __ thee," hand
   over thy cloak also (Matt. 5:40)
9 Chewbacca's partner (2 words)
10 "My people will live…in secure
   __" (Isa. 32:18 NIV)
11 Daniel written about this time
12 Part of image made of brass
   (Dan. 2:32)
13 The Lord "looketh to the __ of
   the earth" (Job 28:24)
21 Alps need, for many
23 Signaling trees of
   1 Chronicles 14:15
25 Full box
26 Where papyrus grows
27 Run to strong tower to be __
28 Locust covered every __ of Egypt
29 Angel said, "__ not, Daniel"
   (Dan. 10:12)

30 Ancient of Days robe color
32 Times per day Daniel prayed
33 Mets' former ballpark
34 British politician William
35 Hormone (Abbr.)
39 Actor
42 Israel making treaties
45 Ashen
46 Impressionist painter
47 Weight measurement
48 Daniel interpreted
49 Joseph said, "Come down to me;
   don't __ " (Gen. 45:9 NIV)
50 Adam and Joseph, informally
51 "We have __ wickedly"
   (Neh. 9:33)
53 Sports channel
54 The Lord is God, there is none __
55 Ogle

58 Psalm writer, __ of music
   (Abbr.)
59 Will Smith biopic

81

RETURN FROM EXILE

ACROSS

1 Nehemiah singers, Sons of __
6 Pilate's garb
10 Cousins of prodigal pals (Luke 15:16)
14 Beneficiary
15 Missing soldier's status (Abbr.)
16 Nehemiah contemporary
17 Jerusalem sacrifice site
18 His sons provided offerings (Neh. 10:39)
19 Person, place, or thing
20 Great Barrier __
21 Aaron's rod topper
22 Walls at Ezra's arrival
24 Mined metals
26 Exile prophet
27 Sacrifice must be perfect, not this
30 Baseball player Ty
31 Calms
32 Shiny balloon material
33 Chicken __ King (2 words)
36 Disturbed, Nehemiah __ in the night
37 God's bow shape
38 Sin offering part (Lev. 4:11 NKJV)
40 First letter of Ps. 23
41 "Will you __ the case for God?" (Job 13:8 NIV)
43 Cabbage, to frau
44 Nehemiah sacrifices
45 Strange person
46 Layer of tissue
49 See 44 Across
50 Exiles' new dwellings
51 Peter __ to Jesus' tomb

52 "There is none righteous, no __" (Sp.)
56 Land unit in Jerusalem
57 "Iron sharpeneth __" (Prov. 27:17)
59 Author Rice Burroughs
60 Nehemiah rebuilt Fish __
61 Moses' temporary home
62 Forest clearing
63 Jesus' torment
64 Gift to rebuild Jerusalem
65 Greek sandwiches

DOWN

1 Month temple completed
2 Bottom of Ezra's foot
3 Before (Prefix)
4 Large Asian pheasants
5 Pronoun for Rahab
6 Ankle bone
7 Payable
8 Joseph's title, for short
9 *Arabian Nights* man (2 words)
10 ___ Matisse, painter
11 Atmosphere layer
12 Porridge
13 Abraham's descendants like the __ of the sea
21 Daniel's sleeping place
23 Condition of Jesus' bones
25 Conducted in labs
26 Offerings of Ezra 6:10 were this (Lat.)
27 How Jericho's walls fell
28 Tempt
29 Perfume plant (sing.)
30 King who helped exiles to return
32 Lava

33 Weeping "was heard __ off"
(Ezra 3:13)

34 "__ Him, all you peoples!"
(Ps. 117:1 NKJV)

35 Psalm-singing voice

39 "A man who has friends must
himself be __" (Prov. 18:24 NKJV)

42 Growing

45 Defeat the foe

46 Central

47 Large artery

48 Swine ran down a "__ place"
(Mark 5:13)

49 Nile tides did this

50 Joseph filled his brother's with
silver

51 Darius read this (Ezra 6:2)

53 Another name for Sinai
(Gal. 4:25)

54 Pedestal part

55 Worshiped in Philippi

58 Kishon is one (Sp.)

59 Child might ask for
(Luke 11:12)

82

OLD TESTAMENT WOMEN

ACROSS

1 Garret
6 Esther's banquet
10 Boaz put Ruth "at __ by speaking kindly" (Ruth 2:13 NIV)
14 Mentor
15 Aroma
16 Ooze
17 Husband of 6 Down
18 First Gospel (Abbr.)
19 Deborah's was a palm
20 Moose-like ark-dweller
21 Lampstand center
23 Pakistan city
25 Arouse, as 2 Peter 3:1
26 First woman
27 "Glorious things are __ of thee" (Ps. 87:3)
30 Attests
34 Mischievous
35 Unclean swimmers
36 20 Across Asian cousin
38 Pinches
39 To be
40 Hebrew night guide (2 words)
42 Fixed charge
43 Describes wilderness
44 Barbarian of films
45 Basketball move
48 Describes 40 Across
49 Wheeled vehicle
50 Mark 4:37 activity
51 Greek wisdom goddess
54 "How can one be __ alone?" (Eccl. 4:11)
55 Delivery service
58 Proper
59 Gray, as Isaiah 46:4
61 Ruth's sister-in-law
63 Cracker type
64 Angels' glow
65 Used to hang Haman
66 Eve's home
67 Ladies' fur coat
68 Matchmaker

DOWN

1 Pain
2 Building implement
3 Woman's work
4 "The breath of God produces __" (Job 37:10 NIV)
5 "For whom the Lord loves He __" (Hebrews 12:6 NKJV)
6 Hosea's wife
7 26 Across's husband
8 His wife turned to salt
9 Dull
10 Woman "for such a time as this" (Esther 4:14)
11 Air (Prefix)
12 Miriam's role (var.)
13 David's weapon (Fr.)
22 Alloy
24 Hail (Lat.)
25 Brief play
27 We must die to __
28 Delilah __ Samson for info
29 "I will __... the sacrifice of thanksgiving" (Ps. 116:17)
30 Eagle's nest
31 Sleigh
32 Fastening
33 Isaac's mother
35 English nobleman
37 35 Down home, perhaps

40 Asperity
41 Thwart, as Psalm 33:10 NIV (sing.)
43 33 Down's husband
46 He delivers 4 Down
47 Disallow
48 Prefix meaning "son of"
50 Deborah's partner
51 Niche
52 Walked
53 "__ me under the shadow of Your
   wings" (Ps. 17:8 NKJV)
54 Esther's task
55 Xerxes "set the royal crown __
   [Esther's] head" (Esther 2:17))
56 Future's opposite
57 Queens stadium of old
60 French "yes"
62 Hind's mate

83

ESTHER

ACROSS

1 Tax time pro
4 Taxi riders
9 Turkish VIP
14 It beautified 46 Down
15 Scorched
16 Xerxes __, "What is your petition?"
17 Bishop is __ to teach
18 Daniel, to Romans
19 Day 46 Down made petition
20 Crawler in kings' palaces
22 "Where can I __ from thy presence?" (Ps. 139:7 NIV)
24 "...for such a __ as this" (Esther 4:14)
25 Abbr. used by 1 Across
27 Lily type
31 Fastener
32 Noah's measurement
33 Nickname for 18 Across
34 Kansas linebacker Jordan
36 Ephod stone
38 Artist Andy
40 God's appearance in the bush (2 words)
42 Car rental company
43 Muppet grouch
44 Lord's is stretched out
45 Xerxes' kingdom, KJV-style
47 Prima donna
51 It entangles wicked (Job 18:8 NIV)
53 Seen before the throne (2 words)
54 Adam's first home
55 Matthew skill (Abbr.)
57 Snippy
59 Water retention
62 Protection, as in Job 1:10
65 Beggar's seat
66 First month to Esther
67 John rebuked Herod for them
68 Roaring cat (Lat.)
69 Esther's banquet, e.g.
70 Redo
71 Persia to Arabia (dir.)

DOWN

1 National boundaries in KJV
2 Tony-winning musical
3 Nissan model
4 "__ away like an evening shadow" (Ps. 109:23 NIV)
5 Purim month
6 "Their feet __ to evil" (Prov. 1:16)
7 NYC time zone
8 Tennis' Graf
9 Head, as Psalm 7:16
10 Mordecai grief signs
11 Winter sport need
12 Pronoun for Esther
13 Who can __ one cubit to his height?
21 "__ from evil, do good" (Ps. 34:14)
23 Abraham's nephew
25 Gasoline or coal
26 Big Blue maker
28 Dutch cheese
29 Mordecai's seat
30 The Lord our God is __
32 Bill Gates role (Abbr.)
35 Audio frequency (Abbr.)
36 Pie __ mode (2 words)
37 Esther's banquet site

38 "Lo, the heavens __ opened" (Matt. 3:16)
39 God's are everlasting
40 Xerxes empire region
41 Agricultural grp.
42 Son of Noah
43 Lyric poem
45 Apple type
46 Vashti's replacement
48 Principles
49 They make up scripture
50 Nevertheless
52 Esther's foe
56 Luke 14 RSVP "I __"
57 Gawk
58 Jews had __ from their enemies
59 Jerusalem to Shushan (dir.)
60 Persian army unit (Abbr.)
61 Aleppo to Babylon (dir.)

63 Mother of all living
64 Criticize (slang)

ACROSS

1 Snare
5 Hindu leader
10 Time period
13 Artery
15 Andrew Lloyd Webber show
16 Sound control (Abbr.)
17 Ruth's field activity
18 Allude, as 1 John 5:16 NIV
19 Ephesus's seventh letter
20 Distress call (Abbr.)
21 "__ people will be my people..." (Ruth 1:16 NIV)
23 Snake's poison
25 Boaz's crop
26 Conductor
28 Event that sent Elimelech to Moab
31 Aplomb
32 Ireful
33 Mouth off
34 Judah to Moab (dir.)
37 Not any
38 "You of little faith...why did you __?" (Matt. 14:31 NIV)
40 College head
41 Pro sport alliance (Abbr.)
42 Data transmission rate
43 25 Across location
44 63 Across did for Obed
45 Grain, as Judges 15:5
46 Assign
49 Axe or hammer, e.g.
50 Rotate
51 The kinsman redeemer
52 Concorde
55 Used in 43 Across
56 Satan's minion
59 Measure of grain
61 "Pray for those who spitefully __ you" (Matt. 5:44 NKJV)
62 Poet Dickinson
63 Ruth's mother-in-law
64 Israel was __ away captive
65 "He __ over the nations" (Ps. 22:28 NIV)
66 "The Lord does not see as man __" (1 Sam. 16:7 NKJV)

DOWN

1 Labels
2 Chocolate candy
3 Greek god of war
4 School supporters (Abbr.)
5 Air again
6 Affirm
7 Peanut butter brand
8 Ruth and 51 Across __ a meal
9 Season when Ruth arrived
10 Happening
11 Helicopter "wings"
12 Davy Crockett battle
14 "__ who wants to be first must be...last" (Mark 9:35 NIV)
22 Miner's goal
24 Samaria to Jericho (dir.)
25 Jerusalem, e.g.
26 Ruth's home
27 Is not, slangily
28 Huckleberry __
29 Middle East dweller
30 63 Across nickname
31 Fuddy-duddy
34 " Eye has not __, nor ear heard..." (1 Cor. 2:9 NKJV)
35 Elisha's head

36 The Lord will judge the __ of the earth
38 Fix socks
39 Depose
40 The sun returned ten degrees on Ahaz's __
42 Construction worker
43 Solidified
44 Neither's partner
45 Ark slitherer, perhaps
46 Describes judgment day
47 Period
48 Longed
49 Belonging to Mr. Orlando
51 Tree trunk
52 51 Across removed his
53 The __ yesterday, today, and forever

54 " __ is my commandment, that ye love one another" (John 15:12)
57 Flightless bird
58 David commanded (Abbr.)
60 Adam, Abraham, e.g. (slang)

ACROSS

1 Keying error
5 Anointed finger
10 Jerusalem to Gaza (dir.)
13 "I will praise thee…with my whole __" (Ps. 9:1)
15 Artist's tool
16 Expression of surprise
17 Defense
18 Carpenter's tool
19 Moses' basket covering
20 God heals when we are __
21 The godly flourish like one
23 See 22 Down
25 Footwear
26 Hates
28 "The way of the __ leads to destruction" (Ps. 1:6 NIV)
31 Witches' group
32 "I have eaten __ like bread" (Ps. 102:9)
33 Eager
34 Deaf communication (Abbr.)
37 The Lord is __ to anger
38 Prize for excellence
40 Veer
41 Spiritedness
42 Indian dress
43 Heavenly lights
44 Ruth, Esther, e.g.
45 Stages
46 Sufferings
49 "I will __ no evil, for you are with me" (Ps 23:4)
50 The wrongdoer's walk, as Psalm 12:8 NKJV
51 "At Your right __ are pleasures forevermore" (Ps. 16:11 NKJV)
52 Energy measurement (Abbr.)
55 Dispensable candy
56 Jacob's father
59 Sandwich cookies brand
61 Downwind
62 Daring
63 Eagle's "arms"
64 Finis
65 Athletic contests
66 Aroma

DOWN

1 Asian cuisine
2 Holler
3 Water carrier
4 Sphere
5 Wigwam
6 Patriot Nathan
7 "Born in the __"
8 Adam, David, et. al.
9 __ be the Lord
10 He stands with wrongdoers (Ps. 109:6)
11 Arrow holder
12 Piers
14 10 percent gift
22 With 23 Across, a comfort
24 Number of lyre's strings
25 Alter
26 Wander
27 "Turn from __ and do good" (Ps. 37:27)
28 Hornet
29 Malta or Cyprus
30 Cut apart
31 Log house
34 Word of woe

35 "The testimony of the Lord is
   __" (Ps. 19:7)
36 James's nickname, with "the"
   (Mark 15:40)
38 "How majestic is your __ in all
   the earth!" (Ps. 8:1 NIV)
39 Iron, silver, e.g.
40 Magi's guide
42 Dirtying
43 Valley of the __ of death
44 Babylon to Assyria (dir.)
45 Psalmist's writing instrument
46 "Keep me as the __ of your eye"
   (Ps. 17:8 NIV)
47 Psalm 23 pastures
48 Seeped out
49 Seraphim wings covered these
   (Isa. 6:2 NIV)
51 To __ and to hold

52 Prep a bow
53 African country
54 Cold war foe (Abbr.)
57 __ of Galilee
58 "Mine __ also shall
   strengthen him" (Ps. 89:21)
60 Nile or Jordan (Sp.)

86

PSALM 119

ACROSS

1 Hertz measurement (Abbr.)
4 "I have chosen the way of __"
   (Ps. 119:30)
9 Before, as Luke 7:27 NIV
14 "For your laws __ good"
   (Ps. 119:39 NIV)
15 Moses' mountain
16 Drum
17 IBM competitor
18 Shirk
19 Pay for, as Exodus 22:16
20 Peter in Paris
22 Patmos, for one
24 Org. with farm oversight
25 Has possession
27 Christmas
31 "The Lord looks down and __ all
   mankind" (Ps. 33:13 NIV)
32 Proverb
33 Buddy
34 "Your __ made me and formed
   me" (Ps. 119:73 NIV)
36 Frown angrily
38 Authorities, __ of wrath
40 Changes, as Hosea 11:8 NKJV
42 The heavens declare the __
   of God
43 Describes ephod's gems
44 Fingerspelling (Abbr.)
45 Vineyard areas
47 *The Seven-Year* __
51 Pig food (Luke 15:16 NIV)
53 Grand __
54 Roman emperor
55 Item for sale
57 Young swan
59 One who counts on

62 "Let him seek peace, and __ it"
   (1 Peter 3:11)
65 Small amount
66 Channel
67 Ridged surface
68 Cyprus to Babylon dir.
69 In Christ all the fullness of the
   __ lives
70 Blow away, as Isaiah 8:8 NIV
71 Color describing Esau

DOWN

1 College grounds and buildings
2 "Let me live that I may __ you"
   (Psalm 119:175 NIV)
3 Separate
4 Russian ruler
5 Rip
6 Jose's one
7 __ Chi
8 "Thou art my __ place and my
   shield" (Ps. 119:114)
9 Cain killed him
10 Bees' production
11 Alpha/Omega, Beginning/__
12 "Long __ I learned from your
   statutes" (Ps. 119:152 NIV)
13 __ Jones Industrial average
21 Thin slice of ham
23 Gilead to Moab (dir.)
25 Chances of winning
26 "Before I __ afflicted I went
   astray" (Ps. 119:67 NIV)
28 "Look thou __ me, and be merciful" (Ps. 119:132)
29 The Lord's are righteous
   (Ps. 119:106 NIV)
30 First letter of Leviticus

32 Industrious insect
35 "Let not __ iniquity have dominion over me" (Ps. 119:133)
36 Daytime light
37 Weeping
38 "Keep your servant __ from willful sins" (Ps. 19:13 NIV)
39 God's Word more precious than (Ps. 19:10 NIV)
40 Crispy squares cereal
41 "He hath set __ love upon me" (Ps. 91:14)
42 Void
43 __ Lanka
45 Investment term (Abbr.)
46 Streams
48 God's mercies are __ (Ps. 119:77)
49 Put a fold in

50 Breeding ground
52 "How __ are your words to my taste" (Ps. 119:103 NIV)
56 Chichi
57 Naaman's desire, per 2 Kings 5
58 Dog's cry
59 "Thy word have I __ in mine heart" (Ps. 119:11)
60 Trinity: three-in-__
61 Greek letter
63 Hebron to Joppa dir.
64 Luke 8:3 woman, to friends

87

THE BOOK OF PROVERBS

ACROSS

1 Squabble
5 Israel was Jacob's
10 Kansas summer time zone
13 Left out of gear
15 Brand of card game
16 Pronoun for Proverbs 31 gal
17 Commoner
18 Poor man might do this (Prov. 30:9)
19 Roberto's bravo
20 Make clothing
21 Lotion ingredient
23 Misses
25 Very strong metal
26 Polaroids or Kodaks
28 "__thy works unto the Lord" (Prov. 16:3)
31 Noble gas
32 Unconditional love (Gr.)
33 Horse control
34 Exceed
37 Sins
38 How trumpet is played
40 Adam or Solomon, e.g.
41 Snare
42 Greek rainbow goddess
43 Grown, as Jeremiah 5:28
44 "Put a __ to your throat if you are given to gluttony" (Prov. 23:2 NIV)
45 Without this, the people perish (Prov. 29:18)
46 Edit
49 Jonah's boarding site
50 It goes before a fall (Prov. 16:18)
51 "Those who __ in wisdom are kept safe" (Prov. 28:26 NIV)
52 Expression of surprise
55 Mo. before Dec.
56 Apex opposite
59 Willing, as Proverbs 31:13 NIV
61 Lamb's mom
62 "__ in the Lord with all your heart" (Prov. 3:5 NIV)
63 Lived
64 "Go to the __, you sluggard" (Prov. 6:6 NIV)
65 Man plans, but God directs these (Prov. 16:9)
66 Jordan's current

DOWN

1 Crests
2 This person will be hungry
3 Seraphim action (Isaiah 6:6)
4 Mo. after Jan.
5 Malicious burning
6 Not early
7 God's breath produces (Job 37:10 NIV)
8 The Preacher, __ 9 Down (Abbr.)
9 Ecclesiastes author
10 Psalm singers
11 D in Corinth
12 Lock of Samson's hair
14 Endearment
22 Abraham's nephew
24 40 Across in a group
25 Demons (var.)
26 Met Jonah at 49 Across
27 Fer's opposite (var.)
28 Adam's son
29 Stare at
30 Thick drink

31 "The sea __ by...a great wind"
    (John 6:18)
34 Cab
35 Tub spread
36 NYC's __ Station
38 Paul's cell (var.)
39 It comes from the heart"
    (Prov. 4:23)
40 Hide
42 Forms a depression
43 Unrighteous
44 Offering animal
45 Tome (Abbr.)
46 Sleep disorder
47 Cattle color
48 Metal bolt
49 Absalom killers

51 Bit of smoke
52 Grandchildren bring joy to
    them (Prov. 17:6 NIV)
53 Stayed silent: __ your peace
54 Pretentious
57 Are, KJV-style
58 "A word spoken in __
    season, how good is it!"
    (Prov. 15:23)
60 Felt in God's presence

88

PROVERBS 31

ACROSS

1 Kung Pao flavoring (Abbr.)
4 Peter's Pentecost preaching, to some (2 words)
9 Locust group
14 Simian ark-dweller
15 Wading bird
16 The wise maintain this (Prov. 28:2 NIV)
17 Actress Dawber
18 Greatest (Lat.)
19 Jacob's post-injury gaits
20 Costly
22 "Write them __ the table of thine heart" (Prov. 3:3)
24 Bunsen burner
25 First Gospel (Abbr.)
27 "She brings him __, not harm" (Prov. 31:12 NIV)
31 Cloud product
32 Israel enemy
33 Creation days number (Rom.)
34 Thinks
36 Proverbs 31 woman might do to her décor
38 Taste buds
40 See 36 Across
42 Awl
43 Proverbs 31 woman is this to her husband
44 Doubting apostle, to friends
45 Expel, with "out"
47 Hoist
51 Job 9:9 constellation (Lat.)
53 55+ org.
54 Proverbs 31 pronoun (Fr.)
55 Ewes' partners
57 Grant forgiveness
59 Witch of Endor power
62 Rahab's cord type of message
65 Time period
66 Breastplate protects it
67 Reduce
68 Dashed
69 "Her husband is known in the __" (Prov. 31:23)
70 "She makes __ garments" (Prov. 31:24 NIV)
71 Cold War–era plane (Abbr.)

DOWN

1 Plotter
2 Ancient Greek city
3 Zodiac's twins
4 Peak
5 Ark of the Covenant carrier
6 Dawdle
7 Lodging
8 "Charm is deceptive... __ is fleeting" (Prov. 31:30 NIV)
9 Sing alone
10 Extort
11 Naval rank (Abbr.)
12 Legislator (Abbr.)
13 Proverbs 31 woman title (Abbr.)
21 "Her __ goeth not out by night" (Prov. 31:18)
23 "Harper Valley __"
25 Silent actor
26 Core muscles, for short
28 "She watches __ the affairs of her household" (Prov. 31:27 NIV)
29 Swine noise
30 "He was despised...we __ not esteem Him" (Isa. 53:3 NKJV)

32 "__ her own works praise her"
   (Prov. 31:31)
35 To listen: give __
36 Reverence
37 Proverbs 31 woman role
38 "She stretcheth out her hand to
   the __" (Prov. 31:20)
39 "Her __ are strong for her tasks"
   (Prov. 31:17 NIV)
40 Invitation abbreviation
41 Cyprus to Babylon (dir.)
42 U.K. measurement (Abbr.)
43 Birds' domain
45 Female animal
46 Scamp
48 "Her husband…sitteth among
   the __" (Prov. 31:23)
49 Third day creations (var.)
50 Occupant

52 "Her children __ up, and
   call her blessed"
   (Prov. 31:28)
56 __ of the Apostles
57 Apostle, for short
58 Thieves' dwelling (2 words)
59 Tiny unit of mass (Abbr.)
60 Expression of discovery
61 God to Abram, "__ thee out
   of thy country" (Gen. 12:1)
63 Kimono sash
64 1 of 12 tribes

ACROSS

1 Wall St. org.
4 Designer Lauren
9 Daniel in lions' __
12 1/5 given to Pharaoh
14 Paul's Athens speech site
15 Shaveh, AKA king's __ (Gen. 14:17)
16 Put on __, as 2 Corinthians 11:20 NIV
17 Train station
18 Winged
19 A merry heart is like this
21 Pacific weather system (2 words)
23 Archer's result
24 Twelfth mo.
25 "Time to __ ...time to hate" (Eccl. 3:8)
28 "I __ vanity under the sun"
31 Fleece in the morning
34 Rahab gave spies one (2 words)
36 Body art (slang)
38 "What profit __ a man from all his labor? (Eccl. 1:3 NKJV)
40 Elijah purified (2 Kings 4:40)
41 To worship
43 Actress Russell
44 Ecclesiastes writer's tool
45 Used to anoint
46 Many Bible land people
48 Luke 14 invitation response
51 Shade tree
53 Feed for Solomon's horse
54 Time period
56 Radio frequency (Abbr.)
58 Abednego's friend
61 Ecclesiastes author

66 Jesus, "My flesh is __ food" (John 6:55 NIV)
67 Alpha and __
69 Insect nursery
70 Makes strong, as Genesis 49:24
71 Fertilizer component
72 "Time to __, and a time to lose" (Eccl. 3:6 ESV)
73 "__ to him who is alone when he falls" (Eccl. 4:10)
74 To exercise
75 Solomon's desire (Eccl. 2:3)

DOWN

1 Fraud
2 Pennsylvania city
3 "Threefold __ is not quickly broken" (Eccl. 4:12)
4 Circle measurements
5 Egypt's representatives
6 Rachel's easygoing gait, perhaps
7 For (Prefix)
8 "Therefore I __ life" (Eccl. 2:17)
9 Surrealist painter
10 Zeal
11 Emperor in Paul's time
13 Greek letter
15 "Time to mourn...time to __" (Eccl. 3:4)
20 Jacob's role for Esau
22 God did by cloud and fire
25 Liquid measurement
26 "What he __ no one can shut" (Isa. 22:22 NIV)
27 When made, must be fulfilled (Eccl. 5:4)
29 Coral reef

1	2	3		4	5	6	7	8		9	10	11

(crossword grid)

30 "Time of ___...time of peace" (Eccl. 3:8)
32 Gideon threshed it
33 Used for tabernacle curtains
34 Smaller than tbs.
35 ___ Schwartz
37 4 o'clock beverage
39 Miriam to Aaron (Abbr.)
42 "Time to be born...time to ___" (Eccl. 3:2)
43 Compact car
47 Job resting place (Job 7:13) (syn.)
49 Leah and Rachel head coverings
50 Before (Prefix)
52 Business venture
55 Not good for Adam to be this way
57 It is deceptively wicked

58 "___ near to God" (Ps. 73:28)
59 Chocolate biscuit
60 A good one is better than riches (Prov. 22:1)
61 An apostle, for short
62 Anti-abuse agency (Abbr.)
63 Joseph's coat had many
64 Goliath weapon (Fr.)
65 Eden tool, perhaps
68 Israel warned not to do with other nations

90

MINOR PROPHETS

ACROSS

1 Investment term (Abbr.)
4 Path
9 Keen, as Zephaniah 3:7 NIV
14 "Diviners see visions that __"
(Zech. 10:2 NIV)
15 Amos's home
16 Explorer Francis
17 Poisonous snake
18 Great ape
19 Bread type (Ex. 29:23)
20 Asian grassland
22 Ephod adornments
24 Cow,-style
25 Sixth month on Jewish calendar
27 Obadiah prophesies against
31 Psalm-singing voice
32 Vigorously (arch.)
33 Torso muscles (Abbr.)
34 Philanthropist H. Ross ___
36 Honey holders
38 Angelic auras
40 Slide fastener
42 Water dispensers
43 Wash cycle
44 Jerusalem to Damascus (dir.)
45 White vegetable
47 Offerings of Micah 6:7
51 Last Supper, e.g.
53 Big cat of Nahum 2:11
54 Eve's son
55 Chances of winning
57 "He leads me __ quiet waters"
(Ps. 23:2 NIV)
59 Internal flap
62 Calf home, as Amos 6:4
65 "Where is the honor __ me?"
(Mal. 1:6 NIV)
66 Stranger
67 Terrible
68 Clairvoyance (Abbr.)
69 Twenty-sixth president, to friends
70 Trinity pronoun (Fr.)
71 __ of judgment

DOWN

1 Mount McKinley state
2 Flower part
3 Turn from sin
4 Cease
5 Was, past tense
6 Jacob, __ Israel
7 Measurement of weight
8 Zerubbabel's prophet
9 Joel prophesied against
10 "__, go to Nineveh, that great
city" (Jonah 1:2)
11 Sarah, e.g., slangily
12 Stretch to make do
13 Horse of Zechariah's vision
21 Lo-Ammi means "not my __"
23 Sea eagle
25 15 Across inhabitant
26 Music storage format (Abbr.)
28 Jesus Christ is the __ yesterday
and today
29 To shorten (Abbr.)
30 Ship initials
32 "For ye __ not my people"
(Hosea 1:9)
35 Corinthian goddess
36 Hertz (arch.)
37 Puccini compositions
38 Sharpen
39 Galilee is one (2 words)
40 God's holy mountain

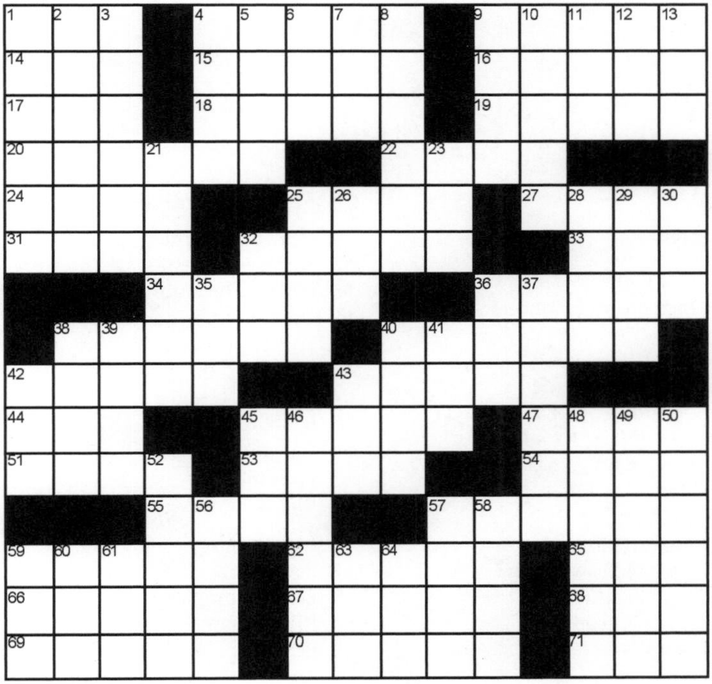

1 2 3 4 5 6 7 8 9 10 11 12 13
14 15 16
17 18 19
20 21 22 23
24 25 26 27 28 29 30
31 32 33
34 35 36 37
38 39 40 41
42 43
44 45 46 47 48 49 50
51 52 53 54
55 56 57 58
59 60 61 62 63 64 65
66 67 68
69 70 71

41 Lodging
42 Garment's edge
43 __ de Janeiro
45 __ Testament
46 Car maker
48 Remained
49 Snake-haired woman
50 Peter in Gethsemane (Luke 9:32 NIV)
52 Lo-Ruhamah means "not __"
56 Peter would __ Christ three times
57 Make unclear
58 Women's magazine
59 Wine holder
60 Lager
61 Chest top
63 "Can __ walk together, except they be agreed?" (Amos 3:3)
64 Ship's back

91

JONAH

ACROSS

1 __ of Patmos
5 Once more, as Jonah 2:4
10 Pull
13 Sleepy, Dopey, e.g.
15 Circle measurements
16 "I stand in __ of your deeds, Lord" (Hab. 3:2 NIV)
17 "Three days __ he will rise" (Mark 10:34 NIV)
18 Tithing spice
19 Joppa to Nineveh (dir.)
20 How God saw Jonah
21 Cain's brother
23 Two-__ sword
25 Potato
26 Deliverers, as Moses and Jesus
28 Jesus in parable, "__ till I come" (Luke 19:13)
31 Days Jonah was in the fish
32 A boundary (2 words)
33 The __ young ruler
34 Downs opposite
37 Nineveh had many (slang)
38 Illustration
40 Jonah's wife (Ger.)
41 Moses sent men to do this in Canaan
42 Lump
43 Outmoded
44 Jonah rested in this
45 Synthetic
46 "He alone __ out the heavens" (Job 9:8 NKJV)
49 Unruly child
50 Fake name
51 What harpist will do
52 LP replacements

55 How dogs drink
56 Suffuse with color
59 Online communication
61 Organic compounds suffix
62 Trinity pronoun (Fr.)
63 Musical piece
64 Jonah, Job, e.g.
65 It sheltered Jonah
66 Cat sound

DOWN

1 Not working
2 Persuade
3 Early's opposite
4 KJV's before
5 Bowed
6 Ancient France and Belgium
7 Naval rank (Abbr.)
8 See 31 Across (Rom.)
9 Jonah told to warn
10 Type of dance
11 Slave's boss
12 Jonah's head covering (Jonah 2:5)
14 Partly frozen drink
22 Sell's opposite
24 Jonah's wish
25 Phoenix NBA team
26 Jonah's transport
27 Roman doorway
28 Horses' meal
29 Horse's walking sound
30 Nineveh or Tarshish
31 Occupation
34 David killed one (Lat.)
35 Future's opposite
36 Egypt canal
38 "Jonah was exceeding __ of the gourd" (Jonah 4:6)

39 Paul beaten with (2 Cor. 11:25)
40 Nineveh's leader proclaimed one
42 Solomon's pursuit, "__ after the wind" (Eccl 2:17 NIV)
43 Jonah's in-fish occupation
44 Where Jonah's fish lived
45 Time period
46 King of __, a type of Christ
47 Shaping tool
48 Mature
49 Lose blood
51 See 66 Across
52 Sweet plant
53 Prank
54 God is "__ to anger" (Jonah 4:2)
57 Cow speak
58 Energy unit (Abbr.)
60 Eve to Seth, for short

92

HOSEA

ACROSS

1 Gomer served stew on one, maybe
5 Remove covering
10 Deadly wilderness snake
13 Married a harlot
15 Israel must "Seek the Lord __ God" (Hos. 3:5)
16 Pronoun for Gomer
17 Supplement
18 Sound
19 Israel as sand of the __
20 "__, I will betroth thee unto me" (Hos. 2:19)
21 Evils
23 "He turned the desert into __ of water" (Ps. 107:35 NIV)
25 "I will __ their backsliding" (Hos. 14:4)
26 Cart or chariot
28 *Phantom of the Opera* author
31 Hosea's ride, maybe
32 Arena shapes
33 Group Abner oversaw
34 Paul's ship passed this side of Cyprus
37 Fight off
38 Wife of 13 Across
40 Grotto
41 Cable network
42 Arizona Native American
43 French composer Maurice
44 Started, as Phil. 1:6
45 Creators
46 People without color
49 "I am the __, ye are the branches" (John 15:5)
50 Verbose

51 Anointing liquids
52 "Time to rend...time to __" (Eccl. 3:7)
55 Israel's enemy
56 Dress, as 1 Tim. 2:9
59 Alpha opposite
61 Made in the __
62 Type of race
63 Humid
64 "I __ them with cords of human kindness" (Hos. 11:4 NIV)
65 "They that __ under his shadow shall return" (Hos. 14:7)
66 It grows on trees

DOWN

1 Pronoun for children of Israel
2 Ruled over Palestine
3 Jonah on the boat
4 Yearning
5 Calves' home
6 "__ saith the Lord" (Ex. 4:22)
7 Fair-weather evening sky
8 Trinity number (Rom.)
9 Hosea job title
10 American Heart __ (Abbr.)
11 Turtle's home
12 Pea (Old English)
14 Paul said them at Ephesus (Fr.)
22 Lazy, as Jer. 48:10 NIV
24 Gomer received from men
25 "__ firmly to the word..." (1 Cor. 15:2 NIV)
26 Wind pointer
27 Middle East head of state
28 Where Eutychus fell from
29 "I will __ betroth thee unto me in faithfulness" (Hos. 2:20)

30 Harangue
31 Tithing spice (Matt. 23:23 NIV)
34 Hosea commanded to do
35 Always, as Hos. 2:19
36 Forbidden seafood
38 Sixties dancing girl (2 words)
39 Musical composition
40 Baked offering
42 Chickens' home (2 words)
43 "I will __ them from...the grave" (Hos. 13:14)
44 Peter, "__ me come unto thee on the water" (Matt. 14:28)
45 Measurement unit (Abbr.)
46 Day of the Lord descriptor
47 Free, as Matt. 18:18
48 See 24 Down
49 LP material
51 Israel history, at first

52 Lily variety
53 Nest occupants
54 "The __ of the Lord are right" (Hos. 14:9)
57 Israel's goodness compared to (Hos. 6:4)
58 Southern university, __ Miss
60 Gomer to Lo-Ammi (var.)

93

OLD TESTAMENT PLANTS

ACROSS

1 Baby Esau called Isaac
5 Ancient Indian
10 Unclean rodent
13 Warning
15 Body of Christ
16 Satan's was large
17 Absurd
18 Remove lid
19 Small gulf
20 "Yet in my flesh shall I __ God" (Job 19:26)
21 Depend
23 Egypt to Red Sea was one
25 Volcano
26 Skirt type
28 Crop's home (2 words)
31 Brush off
32 The Word of God
33 Lubricants
34 Diet Coke precursor
37 Shield (var.)
38 Jesus said, "__ I tell you…" (Luke 23:33)
40 Sin, slangily (2 words)
41 Hallucinogen (Abbr.)
42 "He…is greater __ he who is in the world" (1 John 4:4)
43 Debates (arch.)
44 One sheltered Jonah
45 Egyptian food
46 Pacify
49 Date grower
50 Bible land legumes
51 Part of ark window, maybe
52 Expression of surprise
55 Smack
56 Statement of faith
59 Wilderness resting spot
61 "The voice of __ crying in the wilderness" (John 1:23)
62 Time period
63 Artist Andrew
64 Type of 24 Down
65 Kings' Joshua 9 trick: don __ clothes
66 "My yoke is __…my burden is light" (Matt 11:30)

DOWN

1 Adam, Jacob, et. al. slangily
2 Healing plant
3 Palm fruit
4 Are, KJV-style
5 Bird claw part
6 Buffoonish
7 __ Tac Toe
8 Seventh letter in Corinth alphabet
9 Bible land tree
10 Disprove
11 Ephod stone
12 Played
14 Evergreen tree
22 Alpha/omega, beginning/__
24 Acorn producer
25 Snaky fish
26 Short epistle (Abbr.)
27 __ of the Valley
28 Cain's brother
29 Bible land fruits
30 As previously cited (Lat.)
31 God will heal every __
34 Working implement
35 Negative (prefix)
36 Pear type
38 One of two crucified with Jesus

<table>
<tr>
<td>1</td><td>2</td><td>3</td><td>4</td><td></td><td>5</td><td>6</td><td>7</td><td>8</td><td>9</td><td></td><td>10</td><td>11</td><td>12</td>
</tr>
<tr>
<td>13</td><td></td><td></td><td></td><td>14</td><td></td><td>15</td><td></td><td></td><td></td><td></td><td>16</td><td></td><td></td>
</tr>
<tr>
<td>17</td><td></td><td></td><td></td><td></td><td></td><td>18</td><td></td><td></td><td></td><td></td><td>19</td><td></td><td></td>
</tr>
<tr>
<td>20</td><td></td><td></td><td></td><td>21</td><td>22</td><td></td><td></td><td></td><td>23</td><td>24</td><td></td><td></td><td></td>
</tr>
<tr>
<td></td><td></td><td></td><td>25</td><td></td><td></td><td></td><td>26</td><td>27</td><td></td><td></td><td></td><td></td><td></td>
</tr>
<tr>
<td>28</td><td>29</td><td>30</td><td></td><td></td><td></td><td>31</td><td></td><td></td><td></td><td></td><td></td><td></td><td></td>
</tr>
<tr>
<td>32</td><td></td><td></td><td></td><td></td><td>33</td><td></td><td></td><td></td><td>34</td><td>35</td><td>36</td>
</tr>
<tr>
<td>37</td><td></td><td></td><td>38</td><td>39</td><td></td><td></td><td></td><td>40</td><td></td><td></td><td></td>
</tr>
<tr>
<td>41</td><td></td><td></td><td>42</td><td></td><td></td><td></td><td>43</td><td></td><td></td><td></td>
</tr>
<tr>
<td></td><td></td><td>44</td><td></td><td></td><td></td><td>45</td><td></td><td></td><td></td><td></td>
</tr>
<tr>
<td>46</td><td>47</td><td>48</td><td></td><td></td><td>49</td><td></td><td></td><td></td><td></td>
</tr>
<tr>
<td>50</td><td></td><td></td><td></td><td>51</td><td></td><td></td><td>52</td><td>53</td><td>54</td>
</tr>
<tr>
<td>55</td><td></td><td></td><td>56</td><td>57</td><td>58</td><td></td><td>59</td><td>60</td><td></td>
</tr>
<tr>
<td>61</td><td></td><td></td><td>62</td><td></td><td></td><td></td><td>63</td><td></td><td></td>
</tr>
<tr>
<td>64</td><td></td><td></td><td>65</td><td></td><td></td><td></td><td>66</td><td></td><td></td>
</tr>
</table>

39 "Lips that speak knowledge are a __ jewel" (Prov. 20:15 NIV)

40 Criterion

42 Bread crisper

43 Bible land flowering herb

44 Weapon

45 Ruth or Mary, e.g. (slang)

46 Loathe

47 Paris river

48 Filled

49 Spongy

51 Christianity, at first

52 Galilee is one (2 words)

53 Punches

54 Like Sodom and Gomorrah

57 Group dealing with MPH (Abbr.)

58 "And forget __ all His benefits" (Ps. 103:2)

60 Sailors' "yes"

94

MEALTIME

ACROSS

1 NE state
5 Paul shipwreck site
10 Food energy (Abbr.)
13 Shepherd "guides me __ the right paths (Ps. 23:3 NIV)
15 "I will __ thee, O Lord" (Ps. 30:1)
16 Trinity: three-in-__
17 Naaman became one (2 Kings 5:1)
18 Data transfer device
19 Isaac: son of Sarah's old __
20 Enemy of Israel
21 After awhile, to Shakespeare
23 Wicked's fate: __ darkness
25 Baths
26 Jacob gave Esau some (Gen. 25:34 NIV)
28 Grain
31 Typographic character
32 Sandwich cookies brand
33 Unclean ocean-dweller
34 Resort hotel
37 Lump
38 Play part
40 Number of Ezekiel's living creatures
41 "Let us __ aside every weight" (Heb. 12:1)
42 Particle
43 For better or __
44 Do-__
45 Genealogies record these
46 Jesus "is __ at the right hand of the throne of God" (Heb. 12:2) (2 words)
49 Land of __ and honey

50 Frenchman's Tuesday
51 Promised Land fruits
52 Sheep mom
55 First cook
56 Transferred image
59 Type of oil
61 Downwind
62 Music used as practice
63 Lowest point
64 Hallucinogen (Abbr.)
65 Palm fruits
66 Bird of peace

DOWN

1 Prodigal's dinner
2 Tub spread
3 No
4 Joppa to Nineveh (dir.)
5 Short notes
6 Nerve fiber
7 Ford model
8 Anointed digit
9 Nut types
10 Raccoon-like animal
11 Heavenly messenger
12 Jeers
14 See 51 Across
22 3 Down, KJV-style
24 Colorado tribe
25 Slit
26 Legal claim
27 Pronoun for Esther (Fr.)
28 Pottage holder
29 Cyrus's was Persia
30 "My God on whom I can __" (Ps. 59:17 NIV)
31 Swarms

34 Noah loaded "two of every __"
   (Gen. 7:9)
35 Force
36 War god at Corinth
38 Savory dish
39 Cob vegetable
40 Utensil
42 Evaded, as 1 Samuel 18:11
43 Comedian Flip
44 Mismatched
45 Describes 8 Down
46 Isaac knew Esau by this
47 Temple roofs (1 Kings 7:9 NIV)
48 At bay
49 "Go with them two __"
   (Matt. 5:41 NIV)

51 Deteriorate
52 Prank
53 Tel __
54 Meager
57 Terminal abbr.
58 Sliced
60 Male child, KJV-style

95

OLD TESTAMENT PLACES

ACROSS

1 Cut
5 Pharaoh's daughter walked __ the riverbank
10 Cedar's "blood"
13 Sound when Elisha raised boy
15 Jonah's under-gourd attitude
16 Number of ribs to make Eve (Sp.)
17 Razor-like
18 Saying
19 African antelope
20 May be clay or bronze
21 Esau's land
23 "__ up a child in the way he should go" (Prov. 22:6)
25 Tiny ark flyer
26 Taught
28 The Promised Land
31 Church governing group
32 Holds 20 Across
33 Bearded or Dutch
34 Prompt
37 Ear or liver part
38 Belief
40 Tang promoters (Abbr.)
41 Israel split into __ kingdoms
42 28 Across city
43 Sky flyers
44 Philosopher Rousseau
45 Berate (2 words)
46 Large weapon
49 Esther's garden party
50 More adept
51 Peter's catch
52 Ephod decoration
55 "Is any thing __ hard for the Lord?" (Gen. 18:14)
56 Lombard's love
59 Wear away
61 Small dwelling
62 Colder
63 Small kin to 46 Across
64 Swine's home
65 Treed (2 words)
66 Nuance

DOWN

1 Door fastener
2 Sound heard in ruins
3 "__ is man, that thou art mindful of him?" (Ps. 8:4)
4 Neither's partner
5 Wicked land of Amos 1:13
6 Weaver's need
7 Choose
8 51 Across need
9 Machpelah, et. al. (poet.)
10 Cane product
11 Orphaned redhead
12 British currency
14 Musical productions
22 Lion's home
24 Pole
25 Get smaller
26 Hiram's land
27 Dimension
28 Jesus' Palm Sunday ride
29 Promise (2 words)
30 With 31 Down, biblical mounts
31 See 30 Down
34 Comedian Reiner
35 Meat-grading org.
36 Magi's starting point
38 Target of 46 Across
39 Post-exile prophet

40 Egyptian river
42 Peach state
43 Jacob's altar site (Gen. 35)
44 Garden of Eden tool
45 Ruth's answer to Boaz
46 OT measures
47 Regarding
48 Polish monetary unit
49 Describes wilderness serpents
51 Pet tormenter
52 Sixties dancer (2 words)
53 Mankind's first home
54 "How can __ mortals prove
   their innocence before God?"
   (Job 9:2 NIV)
57 May be violence or kindness
58 Shirt protector
60 Groove

96

ENEMIES

ACROSS

1 Spinning toy (2 words)
5 Burt offering, a sweet __
10 Situps target (Abbr.)
13 Venomous snake
15 Empties, as Amos 5:8 NIV
16 Nehemiah shook as a sign
17 Town __, announcer of old
18 You do not receive, because you ask __
19 Frozen water
20 First letter of tabernacle
21 City paired with 65 Across
23 Alaskan territory
25 Voucher for a small debt
26 Eden deceiver
28 Incite, as Amos 6:14 NIV (2 words)
31 Fertile desert area
32 Lowest point
33 Cocooned insect
34 Cooking measure (Abbr.)
37 Gideon's Midianite foe
38 Meat offering frequency
40 Secure, as Esther 8:8
41 Constrictor snake
42 Swiss capital
43 End, as Ezra 5:5
44 Be holy and without __
45 Fought Asa in 1 Kings 15
46 Lion descriptor
49 More's opposite
50 Persian king
51 "Your redemption draweth __" (Luke 21:28)
52 Prefix meaning "daughter of" (Heb.)
55 __ Fool's Day (Abbr.)
56 Job's foe
59 "Let us make man in our __" (Gen 1:26)
61 "Is anything __ hard for the Lord?" (Gen. 18:14)
62 Excite
63 Abigail's husband
64 Jezreel to Samaria (dir.)
65 City paired with 21 Across
66 David used to soothe Saul

DOWN

1 Ledger (Abbr.)
2 Grieving, Jacob __ his clothes
3 Off-Broadway award
4 Before (Prefix)
5 Separate
6 Israel's oppressor
7 French "yes"
8 Sarah to Abraham (Abbr.)
9 Jonah's destination
10 Similar
11 Breakfast meat
12 Used
14 Camelot's king
22 Shrill bark
24 Delivery service
25 Manger, as Job 39:9
26 Israel's first king
27 Caleb sent to "__ out the land" (Josh. 14:7)
28 Stuck-up person
29 Tropical edible root
30 Notion
31 State as an opinion
34 Chamomile, Green, e.g.
35 Priestly garment piece
36 Supplication

38 Do with, as Ruth 1:17 NIV
39 David's fighting force
40 Red, Galilee, e.g.
42 "The Lord __ his people with peace" (Ps. 29:11 NIV)
43 Redeem (2 words)
44 Heat measurement (Abbr.)
45 Plead, as Esther 4:8 NIV
46 Gets out
47 Misspellings, etc.
48 Jehoram slain with one
49 Fine fabric
51 Multi-national military alliance (Abbr.)
52 Moses, Samuel, e.g.
53 Another name for Sinai
54 From a distance (comb. form)
57 Forty Thieves' guy __ Baba
58 Later apostle, to friends

60 Last OT book (Abbr.)

97

MIRACLES

ACROSS

1 Jordan river conveyance, perhaps
5 Improvise a speech (2 words)
10 It held widow's oil
13 With
15 Devil's "walk"
16 Gaza to Hebron (dir.)
17 Raccoon-like animal
18 Sin, slangily
19 Jesus walked on __ of Galilee
20 Unclean seafood
21 Garlic "container"
23 Mulberry tree miracle (2 Sam. 5:24)
25 Behold, it was __ good
26 Asserts
28 Expelled demon name (Mark 5:9)
31 Elisha's seat
32 Moses' brother
33 Seethe
34 Boxer Muhammad
37 Israel's early history
38 Pillow covers
40 Modern-day Persia
41 Describes Satan
42 Blessing
43 Spasm
44 Nile turned into this
45 __ Scholar
46 Moses' staff turned into this
49 Night light
50 Decorates
51 Extinct bird
52 Parting of the __ Sea
55 European sea eagle
56 Separate
59 Nazarite no-no
61 Goddess in Thessalonika
62 Israel was sent into __
63 Ox harnesses
64 Before (Prefix)
65 Jesus said, "Peace, be __. And the wind ceased" (Mark 4:39)
66 Fringe benefit

DOWN

1 "The __ is not to the swift" (Eccl. 9:11)
2 Planted by the Lord (sing.)
3 Jesus' ride (Matt. 21:5)
4 Explosive (Abbr.)
5 Ably
6 Colorless
7 Throw
8 Pacific island, __ Jima
9 With 45 Down, Aaron's miracle
10 Chief miracle-worker
11 Concerning
12 Digests words
14 Sun-stilled site (Josh. 10:12)
22 Water-to-wine holder
24 Widow's multiplied
25 Stringed instrument (var.)
26 Object
27 Opp. of yesses
28 Vietnam neighbor
29 __ Grey tea
30 Older Jacob's hair color
31 "...and having done all, to __" (Eph. 6:13)
34 Describes wilderness
35 Ephod tie
36 Used with 54 Down
38 Anon
39 Owl sound

40 Elisha made it float
42 Uplifts
43 Picky
44 Heart rate (Abbr.)
45 Pole
46 See 9 Down
47 Fault
48 Cleanse
49 Mushroom type
51 Kidron or Eshcol
52 Field tool
53 Always, as Psalm 25:15
54 Scribe's work area
57 Phone line (abbr.)
58 Caesar's seven
60 Skip and jump partner

98

NAMES OF GOD

ACROSS

1 Annapolis, U.S. Naval __ (Abbr.)
5 Opposed
9 Spicy condiment
14 Esther's banquet
15 __ of the woman
16 Animal's nose
17 Blind guides "strain at a __"
   (Matt. 23:24)
18 Unclean hopper
19 Heron
20 "__has sent me" (Ex. 3:14)
   (2 words)
21 Airport landing area
23 Nile whirlpool
24 Hebrew name for God
26 Jonathan to David (slang)
28 "The Lord our God is __"
29 Sacrificial lamb would not
   have one
31 Latin greeting
34 Write later time
37 Female horses
39 __ of the host of the Lord
   (Abbr.)
40 Mighty __
41 Time Jesus was crucified
42 Tend to, as Genesis 2:15
44 Where birds fly
47 __ Commandments
48 Encourage
50 Billion years
51 Egypt to Israel (dir.)
52 Abba, __
56 *Waltons* creator Hamner
59 Dot __ (printer)
63 First woman
64 Baton action

66 Weapon metal
67 Modern name for Persia
68 Sins, slangily, (2 words)
69 Trick, as Joshua 9:4 NIV
70 Traveled by camel
71 Chilly
72 Samuel and Zadok role
73 Him who __ no sin

DOWN

1 Ephod stone, slangily
2 Irrigation ditch
3 "Remember the __"
4 Music storage format (Abbr.)
5 Guilty, as Psalm 25:2
6 Draw __ to God
7 Time in office
8 Thought
9 Megiddo to Samaria (dir.)
10 __ of the Lord
11 King of kings, __ of lords
12 Took to court
13 Lawyer (Abbr.)
21 Color
22 Bean counter (Abbr.)
25 Lord of __
27 The Lord redeems with His
   (Ex. 6:6)
29 Cooking area
30 Surrender
31 Opera solo
32 Peddle
33 Samaria to Jerusalem (dir.)
34 Cut, as Deuteronomy 21:12
35 He shall __ ; none shall shut
36 Aghast
38 Concerning
39 TX summer time zone

43 __ of Righteousness
45 His fire purifies
46 69 Across synonym
49 Sleep type (Abbr.)
51 God who sees (2 words) (Heb.)
53 Wading bird
54 Circumvent
55 "__ a right spirit within me"
   (Ps. 51:10)
56 Italian volcano
57 Mil. absence
58 Status symbol in Bible times
60 Ventilates
61 He is Faithful and __
62 __ of Sharon
65 Psychotropic drug (Abbr.)
67 Annoy

99

MESSIAH

ACROSS

1 Copied
5 Buccaneers city
10 Before, KJV-style
13 Lion of __
15 Ad
16 "The eyes of the Lord __ to and fro…" (2 Chron. 16:9)
17 Having wings
18 Aging
19 Card game
20 LP speed
21 "Let him __ himself, and take up his cross" (Matt. 16:24)
23 Molded salad
25 Leer at
26 Unyoke oxen
28 OT prophet
31 Describes Bible lands people
32 Improve
33 Steered Galilee craft
34 Canaan to Egypt (dir.)
37 Priestly leader
38 Describes Ehud
40 Lotion ingredient
41 Mozart's "__ Giovanni"
42 Horse command
43 Messiah's is fruitful (Isa. 10:18)
44 Messiah rose this day
45 Totter
46 "Do not be wise in your own __" (Rom. 12:16 NKJV)
49 Give
50 Sculpture types
51 "Into thine __ I commit my spirit" (Ps. 31:5)
52 Santa's helper
55 Baseball stat
56 Prep dough
59 __ Lauder cosmetics
61 "__, though I walk through the valley of the shadow of death…" (Ps. 23:4)
62 Pursue, as 1 Peter 3:11
63 Esau's color (Fr.)
64 Part of a min.
65 "The Word was made flesh, and __ among us" (John 1:14)
66 Book of Numbers contains many (sing.)

DOWN

1 It will hold widow's oil (2 words)
2 Fruit interior
3 Dutch cheese
4 Recording medium (Abbr.)
5 Steak type
6 Partner
7 Blindness "cure" (John 9:6 NIV)
8 Before (Prefix)
9 OT patriarch
10 Burst out
11 Having a secret meaning
12 Prophet who walked with God
14 Protected, as Psalm 139:5 NKJV
22 First letter of Lamentations
24 Transgression
25 Swine's "hello"
26 Wields
27 Egypt river
28 Messiah raised from the __
29 David's army need, slangily
30 Light-producing gas
31 "After I have risen, I will go __ of you into Galilee" (Mark 14:28 NIV)

34 Messiah's blood was __
35 Jacob, "First __ me your birth right." (Gen. 25:31 NIV)
36 Way to cross Jordan River
38 Buckeye State
39 Messiah was __ of a virgin
40 Messiah pierced here
42 Carried away
43 Manger "'food'"
44 Holy Spirit power like (Abbr.)
45 __ Commandments
46 "Whoever __ your word will never taste death" (John 8:52 NIV)
47 Make into sauce
48 Jacob's father
49 Trainee
51 Drag, as in John 21:6 NIV
52 Decorative needle case

53 Messiah's were not broken
54 Messiah's were pierced
57 Masada to Bethlehem dir.
58 Jerusalem to Bethlehem dir.
60 Wise king, to friends

Answer Key

Puzzle 1

Puzzle 2

Puzzle 3

Puzzle 4

Puzzle 5

Puzzle 6

Puzzle 7

Puzzle 8

Puzzle 9

Puzzle 10

Puzzle 11

Puzzle 12

Puzzle 13

Puzzle 14

Puzzle 15

Puzzle 16

Puzzle 17

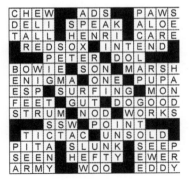

Puzzle 18

Puzzle 19

Puzzle 20

Puzzle 21

Puzzle 22

Puzzle 23

Puzzle 24

Puzzle 25

Puzzle 26

Puzzle 27

Puzzle 28

Puzzle 29

Puzzle 30

Puzzle 31

Puzzle 32

Puzzle 33

Puzzle 34

Puzzle 35

Puzzle 36

Puzzle 37

Puzzle 38

Puzzle 39

Puzzle 40

Puzzle 41

Puzzle 42

Puzzle 43

Puzzle 44

Puzzle 45

Puzzle 46

Puzzle 47

Puzzle 48

Puzzle 49

E	T	N	A		G	R	I	E	F		A	C	S
G	R	A	C	E		L	A	R	V	A		B	O	W
G	I	V	E	R		O	N	S	E	T		A	T	E
O	P	E		R	O	C	K		H	A	S	T	E
	W	A	L	K		O	V	E	R	E	A	T	
A	S	C	E	N	D		C	H	A	R	T
B	O	A	R	D		H	I	S	S		S	O	S
L	O	V	E		I	D	I	O	T		B	O	N	O
E	T	E		S	O	U	L		H	E	L	E	N
	S	A	T	E	D		C	Y	B	O	R	G	
L	A	C	U	N	A	S		T	I	M	E
A	B	O	R	T		M	O	A	N		P	L	Y
B	I	D		A	T	S	E	A		A	D	I	E	U
O	D	E		F	L	O	S	S		L	O	C	A	L
R	E	X		E	C	L	A	T		W	A	D	E

Puzzle 50

O	A	R	S		P	O	N	D	S		J	A	R
A	M	U	S	E		I	R	O	N	Y		E	M	U
H	O	S	E	A		Q	A	T	A	R		S	O	N
U	S	E		S	A	U	L		I	S	S	U	E
	F	I	R	E		V	E	N	E	E	R	S	
S	I	M	I	L	E		D	I	R	G	E
L	O	U	S	Y		A	C	R	E		P	A	S
I	N	C	H		H	A	V	E	S		C	A	N	T
D	A	H		B	A	L	I		S	A	U	T	E
	H	E	R	O	D		P	H	I	L	I	P	
A	M	P	U	T	E	E		M	E	A	N
N	E	A	T	H		W	E	A	R		H	I	M
G	A	Y		A	W	A	I	T		E	R	O	D	E
E	N	E		N	O	R	S	E		R	I	S	E	N
L	Y	E		Y	O	K	E	S		P	T	A	S

Puzzle 51

H	A	D	E	S		R	I	P		D	E	J	A
O	V	A	L	S		E	R	R		J	U	R	O	R
S	E	N	S	E		C	O	O		E	G	R	E	T
E	R	I	E		C	A	N	V	A	S		S	L	Y
A	T	E		G	A	P		E	M	U	S
	S	L	U	N	G		R	O	S	E	T	T	E
L	A	Y		A	B	S		A	E	R	O
J	O	U	S	T		H	I	S		S	L	A	Y	S
O	U	S	T		D	A	M		R	O	E
B	R	E	E	Z	E	S		A	N	D	E	S
	R	O	U	T		E	G	G		D	I	M
O	A	F		O	T	I	O	S	E		D	I	D	O
G	R	I	M	M		E	A	T		O	A	S	I	S
L	I	V	E	S		S	H	E		A	L	O	N	E
E	D	E	N		T	U	E		K	I	N	G	S

Puzzle 52

C	O	M	B	S		A	C	A	D		A	B	B	A
A	G	O	R	A		B	A	B	A		S	L	U	R
B	L	O	O	D		R	I	C	H		K	E	R	I
S	E	N	T		M	A	N		O	D	E	S	S	A
	H	A	R	M		A	M	I	D	S	T	
D	E	F	E	R	S		T	I	E	S
U	S	U	R	P		B	E	R	Y	L		M	E	N
M	A	N	S	E		L	E	E		O	V	A	T	E
B	U	D		G	R	A	N	D		Y	A	R	N	S
	G	U	M	S		P	A	R	K	A	S	
F	A	M	I	N	E		M	A	L	I
N	A	T	I	O	N		S	U	M		A	G	A	R
A	L	A	S		I	B	I	S		G	N	O	M	E
I	S	L	E		N	O	A	H		A	C	R	I	D
L	E	E	R		G	A	M	Y		D	E	E	D	S

Puzzle 53

A	C	H	E	D		A	M	M	O		A	B	B	A
S	H	I	N	A		L	E	A	N		L	E	A	D
E	A	R	T	H		G	A	N	G		L	A	N	D
A	R	E	A		E	A	T		O	P	E	R	A	S
	N	A	V	E		D	I	R	N	D	L	
H	A	G	G	L	E		B	O	N	E
E	X	I	L	E		C	O	N	G	A		B	I	G
R	I	V	E	R		U	N	O		C	R	E	D	O
S	S	E		T	O	P	E	R		H	E	L	L	O
	I	B	I	D		R	E	S	T	E	D	
P	L	A	N	E	D		B	A	D	E
G	R	U	N	G	Y		D	A	Y		A	X	O	N
L	U	R	E		I	R	I	S		D	R	I	V	E
E	D	E	N		N	I	L	E		I	C	I	E	R
N	E	S	T		G	O	L	D		T	H	I	R	D

Puzzle 54

A	P	P	A	L		A	L	P	O		C	R	I	B
C	R	A	N	E		L	I	E	U		L	A	N	E
M	O	T	T	O		G	N	A	T		O	V	E	N
E	P	E	E		D	I	E		D	I	V	E	R	T
	L	E	A	D		R	O	D	E	N	T	
I	D	I	O	C	Y		S	H	O	E
R	A	S	P	S		O	P	E	R	A		R	P	M
I	S	L	E	T		B	A	T		T	I	A	R	A
S	H	E		A	V	E	R	T		I	N	G	O	T
	T	U	S	K		L	O	C	U	S	T	
A	W	H	I	L	E		M	E	N	U
D	I	R	E	C	T		R	A	T		B	E	A	R
O	D	O	R		U	N	I	T		S	A	M	B	A
V	E	T	O		R	O	T	E		A	T	I	L	T
E	D	E	N		E	W	E	R		C	E	R	E	S

Puzzle 55

Puzzle 56

Puzzle 57

Puzzle 58

Puzzle 59

Puzzle 60

Puzzle 61

Puzzle 62

Puzzle 63

Puzzle 64

Puzzle 65

Puzzle 66

Puzzle 67

Puzzle 68

Puzzle 69

Puzzle 70

Puzzle 71

Puzzle 72

Puzzle 73

```
BEAST JOEL  ACTS
ALPHA URSA  PHIL
ALIEN DEPT  PILE
LEAP  AGO CALLED
    HERE SHREDS
ABSENT SEER
HEART DOWSE  WED
ETUDE ARE  STEPE
MAL ROVED  TEPEE
    IBIS VENTER
  STONED GODS
SHAGGY FEW  IMPS
CELL  IRAN KOALA
OBOE  NICE INGOT
WAND  GOES ASIDE
```

Puzzle 74

```
SOAP  ZEBEC  VIP
ANJOU EARTH  ONE
STAIN BRACE  ICE
SOX  BURN  RECUR
   FETA GAINERS
FAMINE  BRUTE
EXERT RUTH   RAW
ELLE  ADOBO BABA
SET OLEO  WATER
   ABACK BEASTS
OUTRANK  MEAL
UNWED  REDS  FIG
TAI ISAAC  EDUCE
ERN ATTIC  LEMON
RYE HYENA   WENT
```

Puzzle 75

```
SHEAF IMPS  SELL
LEAVE NASA  AREA
ARROW SKIM  POPS
BALI  SEE ASIDES
   DEBT CRUDER
INLINE QUIN
ROUND RURAL  PRO
OUTGO OIL  IDIOM
NNE  REINS GREBE
   SALT CHOSEN
  CATERS AUTO
GOURDS GMT  PODS
ACRE  HALE RIVAL
ROAN  OXEN INANE
BALD  TEND OGLED
```

Puzzle 76

```
HALF  HASTE  ALT
AVOID ISAAC  NOR
TONGA NINTH  DAY
EWE  NADA  EARNS
   FIBS TALLEST
AGREES  TEKOA
GRUEL RAIN   SPA
OUST STERN  SCUM
NBE  HERS  ALAMO
   BONES FLORAS
COLLIDE  SLEW
EMITS POUR   BOW
DEN  TEPID TILDE
AGE  EVITA SLEDS
RAD  RENTS  LUST
```

Puzzle 77

```
ETNA  ADLIB  CAP
CHARM GRILL  ASL
HAITI LADLE  CPA
OIL  SNOW  SATIN
   BLOW JUSTICE
DEFIED  FUSEE
UPEND AGED   LEE
NEED CHESS  COAL
SET  PAIN  DOORS
   TONGA TEMPLE
ABSINTH  ROBE
COMET AINT   MCG
RIO  INDUS OPERA
ELK  AFIRE RURAL
SSE  CLEAN  NEWS
```

Puzzle 78

```
ERAS  THUMB  CNS
MACAW EASEL  ROT
MIAMI PLANE  ALA
ADD  COIF  SATAN
   SKID DESCEND
GOSPEL  HAYES
NAKED EYED   HAM
ARID GRASS  NEBE
TSP  POOL  BERET
   WILTS RUBBLE
FRIENDS  AEON
EARTH ESPY   SBE
ETA  OPRAH EXTOL
LET  LOUSE DIANA
SSE  EDGES  IRAN
```

Puzzle 79

Puzzle 80

Puzzle 81

Puzzle 82

Puzzle 83

Puzzle 84

Puzzle 85

Puzzle 86

Puzzle 87

Puzzle 88

Puzzle 89

Puzzle 90

Puzzle 91

```
ISLE . AGAIN . TOW
DWARF . RADII . AWE
LATER . CUMIN . NNE
EYE . ABEL . EDGED
. SPUD . SAVIORS
OCCUPY . THREE .
ALINE . RICH . UPS
TOTS . GRAPH . FRAU
SPY . CLOD . PASSE
. SHADE . ERSATZ
SPREADS . BRAT .
ALIAS . PLAY . CDS
LAP . IMBUE . EMAIL
ENE . NOTRE . RONDO
MEN . GOURD . MEOW
```

Puzzle 92

```
TRAY . STRIP . ASP
HOSEA . THEIR . SHE
EMEND . AUDIO . SEA
YEA . ILLS . POOLS
. HEAL . VEHICLE
LEROUX . CAMEL .
OVALS . UNIT . LEE
FEND . GOMER . COVE
TNT . HOPI . RAVEL
. BEGUN . MAKERS
ALBINOS . VINE .
WORDY . OILS . SEW
FOE . ADORN . OMEGA
USA . RELAY . MUGGY
LED . DWELL . MOSS
```

Puzzle 93

```
DADA . AZTEC . RAT
ALARM . LAITY . EGO
DOTTY . UNCAP . BAY
SEE . RELY . ROUTE
. ETNA . PLEATED
AFIELD . WHISK .
BIBLE . OILS . TAB
EGIS . TRULY . NONO
LSD . THAN . MOOTS
. GOURD . GARLIC
ASSUAGE . PALM .
BEANS . SILL . AHA
HIT . TENET . OASIS
ONE . EPOCH . WYETH
RED . RATTY . EASY
```

Puzzle 94

```
CONN . MALTA . CAL
ALONG . EXTOL . ONE
LEPER . MODEM . AGE
FOE . ANON . OUTER
. SPAS . LENTILS
BARLEY . TILDE .
OREOS . EELS . SPA
WELT . SCENE . FOUR
LAY . ATOM . WORSE
. OVERS . BIRTHS
SETDOWN . MILK .
MARDI . FIGS . DAM
EVE . DECAL . OLIVE
LEE . ETUDE . NADIR
LSD . DATES . DOVE
```

Puzzle 95

```
HEWN . ALONG . SAP
ACHOO . MOPER . UNO
SHARP . MOTTO . GNU
POT . EDOM . TRAIN
. WREN . TUTORED
CANAAN . SYNOD .
OVENS . IRIS . CUE
LOBE . TENET . NASA
TWO . GAZA . BIRDS
. HENRI . YELLAT
BAZOOKA . FETE .
ABLER . FISH . GEM
TOO . GABLE . ERODE
HUT . ICIER . LUGER
STY . ATBAY . TONE
```

Puzzle 96

```
ATOP . AROMA . ABS
COBRA . POURS . LAP
CRIER . AMISS . ICE
TEE . TYRE . YUKON
. CHIT . SERPENT
STIRUP . OASIS .
NADIR . PUPA . TSP
OREB . DAILY . SEAL
BOA . BERN . CEASE
. BLAME . BAASHA
STATELY . LESS .
CYRUS . NIGH . BAT
APR . SATAN . IMAGE
TOO . ELATE . NABAL
SSW . SIDON . LYRE
```

Puzzle 97

Puzzle 98

Puzzle 99

If you enjoyed

99 Bible Crossword Puzzles,

check out

99 BIBLE WORD SEARCH PUZZLES

Paperback / 978-1-68322-753-3 / $12.99

Bible puzzles are a great way to pass time while learning
scripture—and here's a great collection of 99 word searches
sure to satisfy. With clues drawn from the breadth and width of
scripture, *99 Bible Word Search Puzzles* will challenge and expand
your knowledge of the Good Book. All search words
are drawn from the King James Version. . .puzzles include list-
based and scripture passages with search words highlighted
. . .and answers are provided. If you enjoy Bible word searches
(and who doesn't?), you'll love *99 Bible Word Search Puzzles*!